75 Marketing Tips
To Grow Your Business

By Linda Coss

Plumtree Press

A Division of Plumtree Marketing, Inc.
Lake Forest, California

75 MARKETING TIPS
TO GROW YOUR BUSINESS

Plumtree Press/January, 2016

Cover Design by Kevin Coss

ISBN: 978-0-9702785-5-5

Dedication

I dedicate this book to Catherine Balck,
whose friendship means the world to me.

Also by Linda Coss

Three books that have nothing to do with marketing:

What's to Eat?
The Milk-Free, Egg-Free, Nut-Free Food Allergy Cookbook

What Else is to Eat?
The Dairy-, Egg- and Nut-Free Food Allergy Cookbook

How to Manage Your Child's Life-Threatening Food Allergies:
Practical Tips for Everyday Life

Legal Disclaimer

TABLE OF CONTENTS

TABLE OF CONTENTS

Introduction

"Many receive advice, only the wise profit by it."
– Syrus

MANY OWNERS OF SMALL BUSINESSES find that successfully marketing their products or services is one of the hardest parts of their job. This is especially true for those who do not come from a marketing background. Where do you start? What activities should you consider doing – and what do you need to know to make these activities successful? How do you create marketing materials that actually get results? In short, what are some of the secrets to marketing success?

Whether you're just starting out in business or are already well-established, *75 Marketing Tips to Grow Your Business* is just that: Expert advice, presented in a series of 75 easily-digested tips, to help you profitably grow your business.

Chapter 1:
Create Your Plan

"Knowing what you want is the first step in getting it."

– Louise Hart

AS BENJAMIN FRANKLIN ONCE SAID, "If you fail to plan, you are planning to fail." Whether your firm's marketing plan is a simple 1- or 2-pager or a formal 27-page document with charts and graphs, the important thing is to have one. Why? Because your marketing plan is your roadmap for success. Without one you're just "hoping for the best."

Tip #1:
Understand the Elements of a
Basic Marketing Plan

THE EXERCISE OF CREATING a formal marketing plan can help you determine exactly what it is that you want your marketing program to accomplish, how you intend to reach these goals and what yardstick you will use to measure the results.

A basic short-form marketing plan should include the following elements:

- **Business/financial objectives** – What are your business' overall goals? Because your marketing plan will be designed to support these objectives, it's important for you to be as specific as possible.

- **Market overview** – A description of your market, product and competition.

- **Marketing objectives** – What are the goals of your marketing program? For example, you may want to increase sales, introduce a product to a new market and/or increase product awareness among a particular group of people. As much as is possible, your goals should be measurable (i.e. increase sales by 25% by a specified date, increase awareness by 15%, etc.).

- **Target audience definitions** – Who are you marketing to? In addition to all of the people who may want to purchase your product, you may also plan to market to those who can influence their purchasing decision, members of the media, current or past customers and more.

- **Key creative, media and promotional strategies and tactics** – This is the "guts" of your marketing plan, the overall strategy as well as the specific details of how you plan to accomplish your objectives.

- **Infrastructure issues** – Are there any known issues which may impact your ability to reach your goals, such as personnel, supplier or cash flow problems? If so, how do you intend to address them?

While most large companies have a formal planning timeline and process in place, small companies often do not. If you're just "winging it" with your marketing program, a solid plan could make the difference between reaching your goals and coming up short.

Tip #2:
Create Your Marketing Plan

ONCE YOU UNDERSTAND the elements of a basic short-form marketing plan, the next step is to start creating yours. Here are eight tips for getting the job done:

1. **Start with an assessment of past programs** – What worked and what did not? Which programs would you like to continue, and which should be ditched? Do any of your current marketing materials need to be updated or replaced?

2. **Create clearly defined marketing goals** – Your goals should be driven by actual customer needs and values, as well as your business' overall goals and plans. Be sure that your marketing goals are all specific, measurable, actionable and achievable.

3. **Determine your overall strategies** – These are your high-level ideas regarding how you will reach your goals and promote your products or services to your target audiences.

4. **Choose your marketing tactics** – These are the actions you will take to execute the strategy. For example, if your strategy is to become the go-to expert in your field, your marketing tactics might include blogging, creating informational podcasts or videos, speaking at industry events and hosting webinars.

   Note: For more information about marketing tactics, see Chapter 2.

5. **Include a realistic working calendar** – This will help you pace yourself. Include start dates, due dates and responsibilities, always keeping your business' "busy season" in mind.

6. **Create a method for tracking results** – You'll need accurate data in order to evaluate the success of your marketing programs.

7. **Keep your marketing plan front and center** – To avoid losing focus on your marketing programs, keep your plan visible. Write monthly action items on a white board. Put your plans on your calendar. Add your marketing plan to the agenda for your regular staff meetings. And so forth.

8. **Plan to revise your marketing plan regularly** – A marketing plan is a working document. If something isn't working or if new opportunities arise, you'll need to revise the plan accordingly.

Tip #3:
Learn How to
Generate New Ideas

A BIG PART OF CREATING a marketing plan is to generate new ideas. But where are these great new ideas going to come from?

Whether you want for ideas for new products, improvements to your existing products, marketing strategies or anything else, the ability to generate ideas is a skill that, like any other skill, can be learned.

Here are some techniques that might be helpful for you:

- **Define the problem.** What is the issue for which you want ideas?

- **Start fresh.** Let go of your preconceived notions of what works and what's "impossible." Be open to anything and everything.

- **List your pet peeves.** What is it that annoys you about this issue? Chances are these things annoy others, too. How can you improve things?

- **Listen.** Eavesdrop on other people's conversations. Ask your customers what their three biggest challenges are. Look for patterns in what you're hearing, and use these patterns to generate ideas.

- **Get others to ask you questions.** Ask people who are not familiar with the issue to ask you questions about it. They may ask you something that leads to a great idea.

- **Look at other industries.** See what's being done in other industries and think about how you can adapt and apply these ideas to your business.

- **Focus on quantity.** Brainstorm a whole lot of ideas, let these ideas lead you to more ideas, and so forth. Quantity breads quality. Eventually, a great idea might bubble to the surface.

- **Try new things.** Strive to have a lot of new experiences in your life. Try new foods, read something different, travel to new places, meet new people. All of these new experiences will give your mind additional fuel to make the connections that lead to new ideas.

Finally, keep in mind that you don't always have to wait until a concept is fully formed to take your first action. Sometimes you can start with the "seed" of an idea, and see where it takes you!

Tip #4:
Use "Premortems" to
Create Better Plans

IN MARKETING, SMART COMPANIES conduct postmortems after a marketing campaign has run. The postmortem is an opportunity to take a close look at the metrics and discuss what went well and what could have been done differently. In his book, *Enchantment: The Art of Changing Hearts, Minds, and Actions*, Guy Kawasaki suggests that you should also conduct a "premortem" *before* the launch takes place. Premortems can be very helpful for looking at problems in a fresh way. Done well, a premortem can prevent failure by identifying potential problems before they occur.

Get Everyone Thinking about What Could Go Wrong

The basic idea of the premortem is to anticipate everything that could go wrong *before* a launch (or, in this case, before you finalize the overall marketing plan). Assemble your team and ask everyone to think about what you all want to see happen with this campaign or plan. Next, assume the campaign ran or the plan was implemented and it was a failure – and start brainstorming all the possible reasons why the failure occurred.

For this process to work you need:

- **A clearly defined project** – You can't analyze a moving target. What are the components of the marketing campaign as currently envisioned? What is the goal? Who is the target audience? What is the creative? Where will the campaign run?

- **An open and accepting environment** – Everyone involved with this discussion needs to feel comfortable voicing their ideas. They need to trust that they won't be attacked for suggesting how the project might fail.

Take Steps to Prevent or Avoid these Potential Pitfalls

Once you've identified what can go wrong, you need to do something with this information. You may need to modify some aspect of your plans. Or you might simply need to be vigilant about watching for the early warning signs of the problems you identified, tracking each concern through the life of the campaign.

Tip #5:
Avoid Pouring Money
Down the Drain

A WHILE BACK THE NICE FOLKS at Google sent me a beautiful direct mail package. Inside the outer carton was an attractive, high-quality embossed box. Inside the box was a hard cover book, a letter and an invitation to an event in Mountain View. It was very impressive – and a total waste of money. It was all an attention-getting device to introduce the CEO of Plumtree Marketing to a new service targeted at full-service ad agencies. I don't know where they bought their list, but I'm definitely not running a full-service ad agency.

Spend Your Money Wisely

While I realize that marketing isn't an exact science, I'm often shocked at how much money companies waste on poorly targeted, poorly executed or ill-conceived marketing plans and programs.

As you're creating your marketing plan, you should consider adding a mechanism to your planning process to ensure that each program is fully vetted before it is launched. Create a checklist that includes a lot of questions, such as:

- What is the program's goal?

- Why do we think that the program will reach this goal?

- Have we thought through all of the things that might go wrong?

- Are the graphic design, language and tone appropriate for our target audience?

- Is it well-written?

- Can prospects easily tell what we're selling?

- Are the benefits clear?

- Is the offer good?

- Is there a call to action?

- Do we make it easy for prospects to take the next step?

- Is our contact information prominent?

- If this is a mail piece, is the list accurate, recent and well-targeted?

- Do we have a mechanism in place to track the program's results?

- If this is a printed brochure, how and when do we plan to use it?

Take the time to really think things through up front, and avoid wasting money on programs that are bound to fail.

Tip #6:
Use Data to Improve Your Marketing Decision Making

AS MENTIONED IN TIP #2, part of creating a marketing plan is creating a method for tracking results. For example, what's your average response rate, cost per sale and size of sale? Which publications, venues, ads and offers have received the best response? If you've got a gut feeling about all of these things but no hard data, you're really flying blind. And, unfortunately, you may be wasting much of your marketing budget as a result.

Better Data = Better Decisions

Every business should systematically track and analyze responses to their marketing programs, so that future decisions can be based on historical results. What data should you capture? As much as you can! For example, for print ads I recommend that you track the publication name and circulation; ad name, date and cost; offer and coupon code (if applicable); date and amount of customer's purchase; and customer name and contact information (if appropriate). Remember, it's not enough to know that a customer saw your ad in XYZ Publication; you want to know if she saw this month's ad or the one you ran last fall.

Analyzing Your Responses

So what do you do with all of this data? Start by looking at your response rates for each marketing program. This is the number of people who received or had the opportunity to see a particular ad or marketing piece, divided by the number who actually responded to it. Look to see how this response rate changed if you changed the ad, offer, subject line, text, publication, mailing list or other factor. How many sales were made? Compare the average cost per sale and size of sale of each program, and then look at the return on investment (ROI) by comparing the total net sales (or the anticipated lifetime sales to these new customers) to the cost of the program itself.

Think of your historical data as a valuable treasure trove of information, and use it to fine-tune and maximize the success of your marketing programs.

Tip #7:
Put Your Marketing Plans On Your Calendar

CREATING A MARKETING PLAN is only the first step. It's not enough to establish a list of goals and plans. If you want to meet your goals you also have to implement the plans! And the best way to ensure that this happens is to schedule it. Literally. Put your plans on your calendar. If others are responsible for implementing portions of the plan, make sure they do the same. Everyone involved needs to schedule the time to bring your plans to fruition.

Make the Commitment

Putting things on your calendar makes them concrete – a commitment. It also stops you from putting your marketing plan away and forgetting all about it. If you use an electronic calendar system that offers automatic reminders, you should also schedule reminders to pop up at all of the appropriate times.

Don't Just Schedule the Final Due Date

Don't make the mistake of just writing the final due date of a project on your calendar and then leaving it at that. Yes, the final due date should go on your calendar – but you also need to schedule in the work. For example, say you want to send out an email newsletter on the first Monday of each month. Your calendar entries might include scheduling time to create a list of topics that you will be writing about during the year (i.e. creating your "editorial calendar"), scheduling time each month to write and format the newsletter, and then adding a reminder to actually send the newsletter out.

In short, if you want to ensure that your marketing plans get implemented, you need to schedule time to make things happen.

Chapter 2: Choose Your Tactics

"If you have many irons in the fire, some will burn."
– Thomas Fuller

A BIG QUESTION ON THE MINDS of many business owners is, "How can I market my business, increase sales and make more money?" If you're working on creating your marketing plan, this same question can be rephrased as "What tactics can I use to execute my marketing strategies?" Depending on the nature of your business and your budget, the possibilities for marketing your business are endless. This chapter will delve into a number of tactics that may work for you.

Tip #8:
Consider these
25 Ways to Market Your Business

NEED TO GET YOUR CREATIVE juices going? Here, in no particular order, are 25 marketing ideas:

1. **Public Speaking** – Become known as an expert.

2. **Business Networking** – Join some of the networking groups that meet in your area.

3. **Email Newsletters** – Stay top of mind with customers and prospects.

4. **Blogging** – Develop a following while (hopefully) boosting your website's search engine rankings.

5. **Social Media** – Make use of LinkedIn, Facebook, Google +, Pinterest, etc.

6. **Direct Mail** – Send mail, from simple postcards to elaborate packages.

7. **Free Trials** – Give away free samples or no-obligation consultations.

8. **Media Releases** – Try to garner free publicity with a newsworthy message.

9. **Trade Shows** – Have a booth or simply go as an attendee; for some businesses trade shows can be key.

10. **Referral Programs** – Reward your existing customers for bringing in more customers.

11. **Co-Op Advertising** – Join forces with non-competing businesses.

12. **Your Website** – Maximize the effectiveness of your "silent salesperson."

13. **Pay Per Click Online Advertising** – Take advantage of Google Adwords and/or other options.

14. **Events** – Attend or sponsor events that target your prospects.

15. **Telemarketing** – Do some good old-fashioned "cold calling."

16. **YouTube Videos** – Make and post interesting, educational and/or entertaining videos about your products or services.

17. **VIP Customer Programs** – Identify your best customers and encourage them to buy more.

18. **Promotional Items** – Use give-aways emblazoned with your company logo, website address and contact information.

19. **Print Ads** – Place ads in magazines, newspapers or trade journals.

20. **Affiliate Programs** – Get others to market your product or service for you, for a commission.

21. **Signage On Your Car** – Turn your vehicle into a mobile billboard.

22. **Ads On Prospects' Doors** – Blanket the neighborhood with door hangers or fliers.

23. **Online Classified Ads** – Try Craig's List or industry-specific sites.

24. **Article Writing** – Write for trade journals, have columns in local publications, etc.

25. **Free Standing Inserts** – Place fliers in newspapers and/or the mail.

Tip #9:
Use Multiple Tactics

GRANDMA AND YOUR STOCK BROKER were both right: You shouldn't put all your eggs in one basket. This advice also holds true for your marketing program. Successful companies employ a variety of marketing tactics in order to reach their target audiences in a variety of ways.

Plan to Reach Out Many Times

Depending on your business, you may need to reach people many times before they become comfortable with the thought of doing business with your company. In fact, a prospective client may need to notice you, hear about you, see you, listen to you, etc., up to 15 times before they'll buy.

Evaluate Your Marketing Mix

A mix of strategies and tactics will enable you to both reach more people in general and reach some of these people multiple times. Plus, it often happens that a potential client sees the value of what you offer but doesn't have an immediate need at the time. Your marketing mix needs to include tactics that will keep you top of mind for when the need does arise.

While some of your marketing tactics will be ongoing (such as a blog or signage on your car), others will be used just to promote specific events, such as a product launch, webinar or sale.

Look for Synergy

Be on the lookout for ways to make your marketing tactics work together. For example, if you have a newsletter, you can use it to promote an upcoming event in which you are participating. Your display at the event can then include a sign-up list for your newsletter.

Be Consistent

Be sure that your branding and messaging – including your "look and feel" – is consistent across all of your marketing efforts. You want people to be able to recognize that it's you and to become familiar with the products, services and benefits that you offer.

Tip #10:
Nurture Prospects with Quality Content

YEARS AGO THE SALES PERSON was the information conduit between brands and customers. Today, with so much information readily available online, most people prefer to do their homework before contacting you. If you don't provide the information they're looking for – and make it readily available when and where they're looking for it – your competitors will.

Many people say that in today's marketing world, "Content is King." But perhaps it would be more accurate to say "the right content for the right audience, delivered at the right time" is King.

What Types of Content Should You Create?

There is no "one size fits all" answer here. What to create depends a lot on what you're trying to accomplish. For example:

- **To take an in-depth look at a topic** – Create white papers, e-books, manuals, webinars, podcasts, PowerPoints and/or tip sheets.

- **To introduce a topic or address specific questions** – Use articles, blogs, brochures, FAQs, infographics, videos, lists, tip sheets, buying guides and/or product comparisons.

- **To provide credibility** – Consider case studies, testimonials and/or polls or surveys.

- **To address technical issues** – Use manuals, "how to" videos and/or instruction sheets.

What Topics & Questions Should Your Content Address?

A good way to look at this is to consider your prospects' needs at different points in the sales process:

- **Awareness stage** – This is a good time to educate prospects about general questions related to your field, and get them to opt in to on-going communications from you.

- **Evaluation stage** – Show people how your products and services will solve their problems. What makes your solutions superior? What makes your company better? What do others have to say about what you're offering?

- **Purchase stage** – What information is needed to overcome any final objections and get the sale?

Of course, once the sale is made, don't overlook the importance of on-going communication to engage your customers, build loyalty and encourage repeat sales.

Tip #11:
Become an Expert

ALL OF US ARE "EXPERTS" in something. Some keep their expertise to themselves, while others become known as authorities in their field. Your status as an expert can be used to help generate publicity – and profits – for your business.

Your business' goals will determine whether your aim is to make a name for yourself nationally, locally, within your line of work, in relevant online communities or in some combination of the above. What can you do to establish yourself as an expert? Try some of the following tactics:

- **Give talks** – Speak at meetings of community groups, trade associations and any other organization whose members would be interested in your area of expertise.

- **Blog** – Work on establishing a strong voice and following, with the goal of becoming known as a "thought leader" in your field.

- **Publish articles** – Write a regular column or series of articles for your local newspaper or for magazines or websites that are read by your target audience.

- **Join online discussion groups** – Become a regular participant on the most popular discussion boards for your target audience. Be sure your signature line identifies who you are and includes a link to your firm's website.

- **Present webinars** – Contact relevant trade organizations that host webinars for their members, and offer to be a speaker.

- **Write a newsletter** – An informative newsletter can help establish you as a knowledgeable expert. The articles can also be posted on your blog.

- **Write a book or e-book** – If you've been writing articles, turn a collection of them into a book. Even if you publish it yourself, this will make you a "published author" in your field.

Although becoming known as an expert requires an on-going effort, the benefits –increased exposure, leads and, hopefully, sales for your business – can make it all worthwhile.

Tip #12:
Get Comfortable with
Public Speaking

YOU MAY HAVE NOTICED that a few of the suggestions in Tip #11 involve public speaking. Even if you do not plan to actively seek out public speaking opportunities, if you succeed in becoming known as an expert in your field, sooner or later speaking opportunities will arise.

But what if the mere thought of public speaking makes your stomach do flip-flops? Advance preparation – which always makes for a more professional presentation than just "winging it" – is the key. Here are some tips for making your next presentation a success:

- **Learn about the audience** – Find out all you can about the audience, venue and expectations. What is most important to this audience? What is the time limit? Will audio/visual equipment be available (or appropriate)?

- **Narrow down your subject** – What are the five or six issues that someone in this group would want to know about your subject?

When selecting which information to present, ask yourself how knowing this particular information will benefit the individuals in the audience.

- **Make an outline** – List the most important points you want to make, and then organize these points into the most logical order. Start your speech with an attention-getting opening, use real-life or humorous examples to illustrate your points and then end with a recap and, if appropriate, a call to action.

- **Practice your presentation** – There is just no substitute for out-loud rehearsals. Sitting at your desk and mentally "going over" your notes won't cut it! Prepare far enough in advance to allow time to practice – and time – your presentation. Out loud. More than once.

- **Mentally prepare** – See yourself successful giving your speech. Imagine yourself in the room with your audience, with everything going extremely well. See it. Hear it. Feel it.

- **Plan to collect attendees' contact information** – Don't forget to have a mechanism for collecting the attendee's contact information, such as asking the attendees to turn in their business cards for a drawing or to add their names to your newsletter distribution list.

Remember, success is "10% inspiration and 90% perspiration." If you've done your homework, relax and trust that things will go well.

Tip #13:
Network Your Way to Success

BUSINESS NETWORKING EVENTS can be a phenomenal way to grow your business. Countless business owners – from website designers, realtors and hair dressers to business coaches, clothing boutiques, optometrists and more – are all active in networking groups. If you're considering adding business networking to your marketing mix, here are some of the keys to networking success:

- **Identify your target market** – Who do you want to meet? You may want to target potential clients and the people who typically influence their buying decisions, potential strategic partners and other possible referral sources.

- **Choose your networking venues** – Many areas offer a wide variety of business networking opportunities, from industry groups to chambers of commerce, networking organizations, charitable groups and more. Choose wisely, or your calendar will be filled with non-productive meetings.

- **Be prepared** – Bring an ample supply of business cards, as well as some copies of your company's flier or brochure. Be aware that many organizations have each attendee stand up and give a 20- to 30-second "advertisement" for their company; practice yours in advance so your mind won't go blank when it's your turn to speak.

- **Focus on your benefits** – Keep in mind that when you are presenting your business to others you need to focus on the benefits of what you offer. Why should someone do business with you? How will your product or service help them?

- **Follow up promptly** – Within 24 hours you should follow up on all leads, introductions, promises to send information and so forth. Plus, don't forget to send thank you notes to the people who refer business to you.

- **Build relationships** – Networking is all about relationships. Once you've found the right networking groups you should attend regularly, learn group members' names, have one-on-one meetings outside of the group and maintain contact with the people you've met.

- **Bring value** – Be a giver. Help yourself by helping others. Offer free advice or services, look for opportunities to make introductions, refer business to others and do whatever you can to help your networking partners to succeed.

Tip #14:
Use Newsletters to
Stay Top-of-Mind

A NEWSLETTER CAN BE AN EFFECTIVE and affordable way to showcase your products and expertise, and remind both customers and prospects that they should be doing business with you. The big key to success is to put out a well-written and well-designed piece that provides readers with valuable information they don't get elsewhere.

Here are some things to consider before you create your first issue:

- **Purpose** – What are your goals for the newsletter? What do you hope to accomplish?

- **Budget** – Your budget may determine the scope of the project. Enewsletters are much more budget-friendly than printed pieces.

- **Frequency** – You need to strike a balance between staying top-of-mind and annoying people to the point where they unsubscribe from your list. At an absolute minimum your newsletter should go out quarterly. Monthly is generally much more appropriate. I send my business' newsletter out every three weeks, and find that most people *think* I send it out monthly.

- **Distribution Method** – Print or email? Each method has its pros and cons. While e-newsletters are inexpensive and easy to produce, they're also easily deleted. With printed newsletters you have additional costs for writing (they generally have more content than e-newsletters), graphics, printing and postage – but the advantages of a higher open rate, longer shelf life and higher perceived value.

- **Length** – E-newsletters often have just one or two articles. Printed newsletters can be one to four pages or more.

- **Content** – It's generally best to keep the promotions to less than 25% of your newsletter. The rest can be filled with news, informational articles, case studies and more.

- **Audience** – Will this be a "one size fits all" newsletter for your entire mailing list, or will you be writing different versions for different audiences?

- **Responsibility** – Who will be responsible for thinking of the article topics, writing the articles, formatting the newsletter and then sending it out? Who will maintain your newsletter distribution database? Do you want to handle the entire newsletter project in-house, hire an outside firm to manage the project, or use a combination of both?

Tip #15:
Take Advantage of Direct Mail

WITH SO MANY COMPANIES moving their marketing efforts online, mail volume has dropped tremendously. The resulting emptier mailboxes present a unique opportunity. While competition to get noticed in email in-boxes just keeps growing, a well-crafted direct mail package is now far more likely to garner attention than before.

The Advantages of Direct Mail

While both "snail mail" and email allow for targeted marketing, direct mail has some distinct advantages:

- **High delivery rates** – If your mailing list is current, nearly all of your direct mail will get delivered. Email, on the other hand, must get past spam filters, service provider issues and more.

- **High readership rates** – While many people review their email inboxes with their fingers on the "delete" button, studies show that 81% of consumers will at least scan the direct mail they receive.

- **Nearly limitless format options** – Direct mail offers virtually unlimited formatting options, from postcards and envelopes (of all sizes and colors) to mailing tubes and boxes.

- **Much more space** – With direct mail you have as much space as necessary to tell your story and deliver a compelling message in one package. You can include letters, brochures, coupons, photos, DVDs, product samples, small promotional items and more.

- **Extreme personalization** – Digital printing technology makes it possible to personalize every element of a direct mail package, including images, without the expense of multiple print runs. For example, I've seen a college alumni fundraising piece in which everything from the text to the photos was personalized based on the year in which the recipient graduated.

The bottom line: With so much less competition, in some cases direct mail may now offer a higher return on investment than email marketing, even after factoring in its higher cost structure.

Tip #16:
Ask for Referrals

"WORD OF MOUTH" IS THE MOST powerful form of advertising available. The same person who ignores ads, deletes emails and throws away brochures will take notice when their best friend gushes about the fabulous experience they had with your business.

When people are happy with a product or service, they naturally want to tell their friends and associates about the experience. Your satisfied customers can become your "volunteer sales force," spreading the good word about your business for you.

However, even happy customers can use reminders that they ought to "tell a friend." How can you encourage customers to do so? Here are some ideas:

- **Reward referrals –** Create a formal "tell a friend" program whereby you reward your customers for spreading the word.

- **Make referrals easy –** Include a flier about your business and the products and services you offer with each purchase; encourage customers to pass this flier on to a friend.

- **Encourage referrals –** If you have a physical office or store, place an attractive sign in a visible place encouraging clients to tell others about your business. Order a roll of pre-printed "We love referrals" or "I'm never too busy for your referrals" stickers, and place these on your letters, envelopes, brochures, invoices and other printed materials.

- **Suggest referrals** – If you send out regular promotional emails to your customers, add a P.S. suggesting that they forward the email on to others who may be interested.

- **Ask for referrals** – A great time to bring up the subject is just after your customer has expressed their satisfaction with your product or service. "I'm so glad you're happy," you could say. "Do you know of anyone else that could benefit from our service? I would certainly appreciate the referral!"

A positive testimonial about your company – delivered directly from your satisfied customer to a potential customer – is extremely powerful. It pays to encourage your customers to tell their friends about your business.

Tip #17:
Start Blogging

BLOGGING CAN BE AN EXCELLENT way to drive traffic to your website and build your reputation as an expert in your field. It can also enhance your brand's image, give your company a "human" face, allow you to interact with your customer base and provide a great tool for media and public relations.

To build an audience, however, you need to blog regularly, providing content that your readers find interesting, helpful or entertaining. The catch, therefore, is that you need to keep coming up with things to blog about – day after day, week after week.

Here are 21 ideas to get you started:

1. **Interview someone in your field** – The interview can be conducted via telephone or email. Recording the interview and adding audio or video to your blog can be even more interesting.

2. **Write about an event** – Attend an industry conference, meeting or other relevant event and report on the interesting parts.

3. **Reflect on something** – Write about something that happened to you this week, a decision you made, etc. What lead you down this path? What are the implications?

4. **Make a visual post** – Post pertinent infographics, photos or videos.

5. **Review a book or product** – Make it relevant to your blog's topic, and include appropriate links.

6. **Make a list** – Lists (such as this one!) are very popular. 10 Ways to be Successful, Top 25 Companies in Our Industry, and so forth.

7. **Create a how-to** – A tutorial on a popular (but possibly confusing) issue in your subject area will be much appreciated.

8. **Repurpose other items** – Take a look at your company's written materials – website, brochures, documentation, memos, etc. – to see if any of it can be turned into blog posts.

9. **Invite a guest** – Ask an expert in your field to write a guest post for your blog.

10. **Look at the pros and cons** – Examine the pros and cons of an issue, possibly including links to others' posts on the topic.

11. **Do a case study** – Highlight one of your company's successful projects.

12. **Create a guide** – Post a guide to the most important websites and blogs related to your subject area.

13. **Take a historical view** – Write a post about how things have changed in your industry.

14. **Answer questions** – Once your blog has a following you can create posts that answer readers' questions.

15. **Report on current events** – Do a "news" post on what's happening in your field or how your field might be impacted by current events.

16. **Be opinionated** – Take a stand on a controversial issue in your field.

17. **Share secrets** – Tell your readers about generally unknown "secrets" in your industry.

18. **Chart some facts** – Create a pie chart or bar graph that presents interesting facts in a novel way.

19. **Examine the pitfalls** – Write about the common pitfalls in your industry and how to avoid them.

20. **Take a poll** – Invite your readers to participate in a survey, and then blog about the results.

21. **Link to existing content** – Post links to a video, webinar, white paper, blog post or any other content that would interest your readers.

Tip #18:
Give Things Away

FREE. NO MATTER WHAT BUSINESS you're in, "free" can be the most powerful word in your marketing vocabulary. It's the word that no one can resist! "Free" is exciting, enticing and a proven successful marketing tactic. Everyone loves to get something for nothing.

What Can You Give Away?

The possibilities are endless. Here are some examples:

- **Free samples** – Cosmetics giant Mary Kay is great at this. Nearly every time you buy something from Mary Kay, your consultant throws in a sample of something else that she thinks you'll like.

- **Free trial** – Business or life coaches can offer a free trial session; magazines routinely offer free trial subscriptions.

- **Free information** – White papers are very popular in the tech industry.

- **Free advice** – Newsletters can be a great way to showcase your expertise and provide free advice to your prospective clients. Free advice can also be given in person, such as free fashion consultations offered by clothing stores.

- **Free educational seminars** – Take the "free advice" idea a step further and offer a workshop, webinar or seminar.

- **Free gift with purchase** – A plumber can give their customers a plunger, branded with the company logo and phone number. After the customer unsuccessfully tries to fix the problem themself, they'll know who to call!

- **Free products** – Similar to a gift with purchase, except the freebie is your own product. Buy 1 get 1, punch cards such as for a car wash where if you buy 9 your 10th wash is free, etc.

- **Free food** – Back in the 1980s I was a printing buyer. Every time my sales rep from a particular printing business came over he brought freshly baked cookies. I still remember it, they're still in business (no small feat), and my sales rep is now running the company. Coincidence?

The bottom line is that "Free" works. One caveat, though: Avoid using the word "free" in email subject lines, because doing so will trigger spam filters.

Tip #19:
Write and Distribute
Media Releases

WRITING AND DISTRIBUTING media releases can be a great way to garner free publicity for your business. However, in order to get the information picked up by the media, your "news" must actually be "newsworthy."

Of course, media releases are not just a way to get your company's products or services noticed by the media. They can also be vehicles for connecting directly with your target market online. How? Through search engine optimization. Optimize all of your media releases for your key words. Distribute them to the media, and also upload them to your website, where they can continue to attract potential customers long after the "news" is not new anymore.

In addition to the standard media release fare of announcements of new products, new hires or promotions of people within your organization, here are 12 more reasons to create a media release:

1. **Awards** – These can be received or given by your company.

2. **Charitable contributions** – People like to do business with companies that do good. Be sure to publicize your support of charitable organizations and events.

3. **Classes and seminars** – Classes, demonstrations, seminars, speaking engagements and workshops are all good media release material.

4. **Company anniversary** – Invite the community to celebrate.

5. **Contests and events** – If you sponsor a contest or event, use a media release to help spread the word.

6. **Expanded facilities or hours** – Be sure to explain how the expansion will benefit your target audience.

7. **Free information** – Let the media know about the valuable free report, resource list or other information that's available at your website.

8. **Newsletter launch** – Put out a media release when you start up a new newsletter.

9. **New partnerships or strategic business alliances** – Once again, be sure to explain how this will benefit your customers (and not just your own bottom line).

10. **Radio or TV show appearances** – Media appearances are always "news."

11. **Tie-in with upcoming holidays or events** – In addition to the well-known holidays, do some research to see if there's a lesser-known day that ties in to your product or service.

12. **White paper you have written** – Announce some of the pertinent findings of your paper and then let people know how they can obtain the full report.

Tip #20:
Market Your Free Consultation

IN THE RETAIL WORLD, "sampling" is often a very effective strategy. For service providers, some type of "no charge consultation" – either in person or by telephone – can be a successful way to provide potential clients with an opportunity to "try before they buy." It's also a great way for the service provider to "get their foot in the door," qualify the prospect and demonstrate the value of their offering.

What many people forget, though, is that this consultation is essentially a product in itself. As such, thought needs to be given as to how it should be marketed. If a "free consultation" is appropriate for your business, what can you do to overcome the perception that it is just a sales pitch and get people to sign up? Here are some ideas:

- **State the benefits** – Even though you're not charging for your consultation, it doesn't come without a price; your potential clients are paying for it with their time. Make it clear that participants will benefit from the meeting even if they do not choose to engage your services. If possible, specify exactly what will be covered during the meeting, and what information or insights participants can expect to receive.

- **Rename it** – Sometimes saying that you're offering a "free" consultation can lower the perceived value of your services. In this case you can call it an "initial meeting," "no-obligation project evaluation," "complimentary needs assessment," or some other appropriate term.

- **Get others to market it for you** – Create a nice-looking gift certificate for your consultation which others can use as a gift to *their* clients. For example:

  - **A home stager** can create a certificate that local Realtors can give to home sellers upon signing, offering homeowners advice regarding how to better stage their home for the market.

-    ○ **A bookkeeper** can create a certificate for one hour of Quickbooks setup advice that local business attorneys can give to clients who are incorporating.

-    ○ **A wedding planner** can provide a consultation to a caterer's clients.

- **Make it easy for prospects to sign up** – Remember, regardless of what you call it, your offer won't do you any good if prospects can't figure out how to contact you to get the meeting scheduled!

Tip #21:
Maximize Your
Trade Show Investment

EXHIBITING AT A TRADE SHOW is usually a major investment. In addition to the exhibitor's fees you may also incur costs for booth design, signage, literature, free samples, promotional items emblazoned with your logo, travel and more. Even having a table at a local business expo can get costly! Here are some tips to help you maximize your trade show investment:

- **Send invitations** – Let your existing customers know where to find you at the show, and give them a chance to take advantage of your "special trade show pricing" even if they won't be there.

- **Keep an open mind** – While you might have particular goals for your trade show experience, you never know what opportunities might present themselves. For example, take the time to talk to reporters, whose positive write-ups can create enormous demand for your products.

- **Have easy-to-read signage that announces what you do –** Attendees walking the aisles are trying to guess which booths have vendors that can meet their needs. If they can't quickly determine what it is that you're offering, they're likely to keep walking.

- **Be approachable –** Smile, make eye contact and don't be so busy talking with your team members or checking your email that potential customers feel ignored. Plus, be sure that everyone working your booth knows your products and services well.

- **Get the badge reader –** Pay to get the device that can quickly scan the bar codes on your booth visitors' name tags. You'll look cheap – and perhaps too new or small to meet your potential customers' needs – if you don't make the investment.

- **Bring plenty of literature –** Attendees may talk to dozens of vendors, and their minds will turn to mush by the end of the day. When they get back to the office they need something tangible to remind them why they're interested in your company. Be sure your literature includes product descriptions, order instructions and contact information.

Tip #22:
Make Your Business
Visual for Pinterest

WITH THE EVER-GROWING POPULARITY of Pinterest, it's become clear that this very visual social media site is not just for food and fashion images. Many businesses are now finding creative ways to use Pinterest to gain exposure, boost their website's search engine rankings and generate interest.

Considering giving Pinterest a try but don't know what to pin? Keeping in mind that each of your original pins can and should include embedded links back to your website, and that every image should have a unique description utilizing your search engine optimization (SEO) keywords, consider creating boards focused on:

- **Product images** – Including your product itself, your product in use, your product being manufactured or how to use your product (such as the proper placement of a tie clip).

- **Product or service context images** – For example, a company that makes pool care chemicals and a pool care provider can both create boards of beautiful swimming pools.

- **Categories related to your business** – For example, a financial planner can create boards about financial education, whimsical piggy banks or the exotic places her successful clients are visiting on their vacations.

- **Infographics** – These are especially popular for business and marketing topics.

- **Tips or inspirational thoughts** – There are websites that make it easy to turn text into pinnable images.

- **White papers, e-books, blogs** – Show images of your content's cover, or create a call to action pin such as "learn how to XYZ" with a button below saying "click here for more information."

- **Event photos** – From events you host or attend, your community involvement, industry events, etc.

- **Tie-ins to your advertising campaign** – Use the campaign's images and headlines, and then put the call to action in the pin's description.

- **Your team** – Humanize your brand with images of your team members at work (with their written permission, of course).

- **Testimonials** – Quotable quotes from your happy customers.

Happy pinning!

Tip #23:
Seek Out Opportunities
For Cross-Promotions

LOOKING FOR WAYS TO STAND OUT from your competition *and* stretch your marketing dollars? Consider joining forces with another, non-competing business that also sells to your target audience. By cross-promoting each other's products and services you can obtain access to customers and markets you might not otherwise reach, gain marketing resources you might lack, save money and offer greater value to your own customers.

What to Look for in a Cross-Promotion Partner

First and foremost you need to work with a company that's reputable and trustworthy, because joining forces means linking reputations as well. Be sure that you and your potential partner really are after the same target market. Determine if you bring different resources to the table. Consider if this is someone you feel comfortable working with, and try to gauge if you are both equally committed to the success of the partnership.

Ideas for Cross-Promotions

The possibilities for cross-promotions are limited only by your imagination. Consider the following ideas:

- **Give a free gift with purchase –** Your customers receive your partner's product or service, and vice versa.

- **Host an event –** You and your partner(s) work together to create and market a seminar, workshop, demonstration, celebrity appearance or other event.

- **Distribute a combined mailing –** Pool mailing lists and send out a joint promotional postcard, email offer, newsletter or other marketing piece.

- **Bundle your services –** Offer a reduced price, special service or other convenience if a customer buys from both you and your partner.

- **Share space –** Consider sharing a booth at a trade show or community event.

Sealing the Deal

As with any partnership, be sure that you are both clear about expectations. A simple written agreement that specifies what each of you will contribute, including time, money, products or services, etc., will go a long way towards avoiding misunderstandings and making the partnership a success.

Chapter 3: Position Your Products or Services

*"Every brand isn't for everybody,
and everybody isn't for every brand."*
– Liz Lange

HAVE YOU EVER STOPPED to think about what it is that you're really selling? When it comes right down to it, you're selling *solutions* to the problems, needs or desires that your ideal clients have. Does your local gym sell hard work, major time commitments and exercise? Of course not! They sell sexy bodies and good health. Likewise, Mercedes doesn't just sell transportation – they sell status.

"Positioning" is all about figuring out what you're selling, who you're selling it to and how to explain the benefits it brings in such a way that your ideal customers will want to buy it.

Tip #24:
Determine What You're Really Selling

IN REAL ESTATE THEY SAY the three most important things are "location, location, location." In marketing you could say its "benefits, benefits, benefits." Why? Because all your potential customer really wants to know is "what's in it for me?" How will your product or service solve their problems, meet their needs or improve their life? At some level, nothing else really matters.

Understand that People Don't Buy "Things"

They buy what things can do for them. You're selling solutions, not products or services.

People who buy my book, "What's to Eat? The Milk-Free, Egg-Free, Nut-Free Food Allergy Cookbook," aren't buying recipes. They're buying a way to feed delicious food to their entire family, including a family member who is on a restricted diet. This adage is equally true for services. For example, your neighbor goes to the chiropractor to relieve his back pain. His chiropractor is selling pain relief, not spinal adjustments.

Avoid Confusing Features with Benefits

Many business people make the mistake of focusing on their product's *features* instead of its *benefits*. What's the difference? A feature is a fact about the product, while a benefit explains or demonstrates how the product will benefit the customer. For example, "made of heavy-duty plastic" is a feature. "Guaranteed unbreakable" is the benefit of the fact that the product is made of heavy-duty plastic.

Create Different Messages for Different Audiences

Of course, you're probably selling more than one thing. A restaurant might sell "convenience" to one target audience, a "fun evening out" to another group of people and a "way to connect with family and friends" to others. The important thing is to figure out what solution you're offering to the particular group you're targeting, and then focus your message on this.

Tip #25:
Create Your
Unique Selling Proposition

WHEN PEOPLE ARE DECIDING whether or not they should do business with you, there's a good chance they're also evaluating your competitors' offerings. You need to give them a good reason to pick your products or services, and not the competitions'.

What Sets You Apart from Your Competition?

Your Unique Selling Proposition, or USP, is what clearly answers the question, "Why should I do business with you instead of with your competitors?" Often translated into a tagline, the USP should be the basis for all of your company's marketing efforts. You've got to let people know why your products or services are the best choice.

Developing Your USP

How do you determine your USP? Start by finding important benefits that are unique to your product or service. Try looking at:

- **A product feature** – This can be anything about your product, service or service delivery. For example, Folgers coffee is *Mountain Grown.* I think most coffee is mountain grown, but they make it sound unique and special.

- **An emotional appeal** – Perhaps your USP can be based on an appeal to the prospect's emotions, such as love, humor or fear.

- **A possible association** – This is the celebrity endorsement approach. Your product is wonderful because so-and-so says it's wonderful.

Once you have a good list of possibilities, pick one that is unique (i.e. not being touted by your competitors), believable and a big advantage that your prospective customers will actually care about. Remember, this should be something that can be used to motivate people to make a purchase!

Using Your USP

The final step is to boil it all down to one clear and concise sentence and then integrate it into all of your marketing materials. Remember, if you can't figure out what sets you apart from your competition, your prospective clients aren't likely to see any reason to do business with you either.

Tip #26:
Identify Your Target Markets

A BIG KEY TO SUCCESSFUL MARKETING is to tailor your message to your ideal customers' needs. This means that before you can create a successful website, brochure, ad, sales letter or other marketing piece, you must first identify and study your target market. Exactly who are these people? How do they talk, act and think? What challenges do they face? What issues are important to them? And – most importantly – what is it about your product or service that would particularly appeal to this group?

List All of Your Target Audiences

Keep in mind that your business most likely has more than one target audience, each of which has their own particular hot buttons, needs and wants. For example, say you manufacture a product that is sold both to retail stores and direct to consumers through a website. Your list of target audiences might include:

- Potential, current and past customers

- People who inquired about your product in the past but did not make a purchase at the time

- Potential, current, past and inquiring retail stores and distributors

- Influencers (people in positions of authority who could recommend your product to consumers)

- Media (bloggers, trade and consumer publications, newsletters, websites, radio, TV, etc.)

- And more

Tailor Your Message

Rank your list of target audiences in order of importance, and then decide which group or groups you will focus on first. Think about the specific benefits that your product or service brings to these groups and tailor your message accordingly. For example, while retail stores might want to know about your product's compact and attractive packaging, consumers are probably much more interested in your product's durability.

Finally, make sure that everything about your marketing piece — words, colors, overall layout, images used, etc. — speaks directly to your chosen audience.

Tip #27:
Find Your Niche

WHILE SOME COMPANIES TRY to be "all things to all people," most find it much more profitable to focus on well-defined niche markets. A niche market is a targetable portion of a particular market sector. Your goal in focusing on niche markets is to address the specific needs of a specific group of potential customers that are not being addressed by your competitors.

There are many different ways that you can "slice and dice" your overall market into narrow niche groups. The trick is to look for segments of the market that have clearly defined needs or preferences that differentiate them from the market as a whole. Depending on your product or service you can focus on:

- **A particular aspect of your field** – As a marketing copywriter, this is what I do. Although there are many marketing generalists out there that claim to do everything imaginable that has anything to do with marketing, I focus exclusively on marketing writing and editing.

- **A particular demographic** – Try looking at geography, age, ethnicity or other demographic factor. For example, a photographer can advertise as "The Best Photographer in South City," specialize in baby portraiture, or focus on the Quinceniara or Bar/Bat Mitzvah markets.

- **A particular set of needs or preferences** – Niche markets can also be defined by things like price (both Saks Fifth Avenue and the 99

Cent Store sell baby clothes, but probably to different portions of the baby clothes buying market), convenience (think of dry cleaners that offer pick-up and delivery services), or the desire for instant gratification (such as while-you-wait service).

Why target a smaller segment of your market rather than the entire community? Simple: It's more effective, less costly and often produces better results.

Tip #28:
Turn Potential Liabilities
Into Assets

IN POLITICS, "SPIN" IS WHAT TURNS the "inexperienced" candidates into the ones with "fresh ideas," and the "entrenched" candidates into those who "know how to get the job done." In business, "spin" can be used to turn potential liabilities into assets as well.

Sometimes whether something is a positive or a negative is really just a matter of perspective. To illustrate this concept, let's look at some examples...

- **Lack of experience** – Perhaps you just started a business. Some might consider your inexperience to be a liability. Maybe business is still a little slow. How can you put a positive spin on things? You're not "inexperienced," you're...

    o Affordable

    o Flexible

    o Offering a fresh perspective

    o Ready to tackle the client's project immediately

- **High prices** – Not everyone wants to be the low-price leader. But you also wouldn't want to tout that you've got "the highest prices in town"! You're not "expensive," you're...

  o   A highly-skilled expert

  o   In demand nationwide

  o   Providing customized and unique solutions

  o   Catering to those with discriminating tastes

- **"Me Too" Service** – What if you're in an industry where all of the players offer essentially the same thing – or it at least appears this way to the average consumer? How can you position yourself to stand out from the crowd? You're not "just the same as your competitors," you're...

  o   A specialist in a particular niche of the market

  o   The organization with the most longevity

  o   The go-to provider in a given geographic area

  o   The one that provides the best value

Many businesses try to hide their potential negatives completely, hoping that no one will notice them. This approach tends to back-fire. It's often far better to confront these potential negatives head-on, by spinning them around and turning them into positives.

Tip #29:
Transform Ugly Ducklings
Into Beauty Queens

NOT ALL PRODUCTS OR SERVICES are glamorous, easy to get excited about or readily-understood. As a marketing writer, I write about a wide range of products and services. Sometimes when friends ask me about my latest projects, they seem surprised that I can muster excitement about a given topic. What's my secret? Over the years I've learned that if a seemingly "dull" product solves your problems or improves your life, these benefits – and the product that brings them – are anything but "dull" to you.

"Boring" is in the Eye of the Beholder

No matter how unglamorous your product might be on the surface, focusing on the "inner beauty" of the benefits it brings will always make it shine. Here are some examples from my client files:

- **Durable and odor-free commercial diaper pails** – Who can get excited about diaper pails? You could... if you were running a child care center and had first-hand experience with pails that not only leave the entire facility reeking of dirty diapers, but also fall apart after a few months' use.

- **Pre-printed forms for dental offices** – Dental office managers might be hard-pressed to get excited about laser statement forms. But once they understand how pre-printed, perforated forms save money *and* speed payments, the "boring" factor starts to fade away.

- **Medical lien funding** – This is a way for accident victims who do not have medical insurance to obtain immediate funding for medical treatment. To most people, this is an obscure financial product. But for an injured car crash victim who needs surgery *now* – not months or years from now when his court case finally settles – medical lien funding is a real godsend.

- **Telephone & internet carrier services** – A decidedly dull topic...until you find out that there's no extra charge to have an expert manage your business' telephone and internet carrier services for you in such a way that you pay less and get better performance, hassle-free support and an optimized technology environment.

Chapter 4:
Refine Your Message

"The aim of marketing is to know and understand the customer so well the product or service fits him and sells itself."
– Peter F. Drucker

OKAY. YOU'VE CREATED YOUR MARKETING PLAN, chosen your tactics and decided on the positioning for your products or services. Now what? Before you start implementing your plan, now's a great time to take some steps to further refine your message. What can you find out about your customers' buying process? What information do they need to make a decision? How can you best frame your message? What voice would be most appropriate? This chapter delves into all of this, and more.

Tip #30:
Understand Your
Customers' Buying Process

CUSTOMERS DON'T JUST GO OUT AND BUY. Buying is a process, and in its simplest form it goes something like this...First your customers must recognize that they have a problem ("I'm thirsty"). Then they search for information about how to solve this problem ("where's the nearest soda machine?"). They might evaluate alternatives ("maybe I'd rather have coffee"). Finally they'll make a decision ("forget it – I'll just head to the drinking fountain and have some water").

Plan to Tie Your Messaging in to this Process

Understanding how your customers make their buying decisions can be key to creating a truly successful sales process – and the effective marketing materials you'll need to drive it. For example, if you know that potential customers want to see detailed technical specs for each of your products, you can make sure that the links to this information are prominently displayed on every page of your website.

In general, you should try to find out...

- **Process** – *What is your customers' typical buying process?* Depending on your business, customers might obtain purchasing pre-approval, do research, get bids, seek referrals, get financing, etc. How many people are involved in the buying decision? At what point in the process do these other people enter the picture?

- **Information needs** – *What information do your customers typically need in order to make a buying decision?* Do they understand how your product or service will solve their problems or improve their lives? Are they looking for price information? How about reviews from previous customers? Do you need to provide a thorough explanation of how your service works? Will your money-back guarantee put them at ease?

- **Motivation –** *What motivates people to buy the products or services that you offer instead of doing nothing?* What problems can be solved by making this purchase? How pressing are these problems? A person who is looking for the nearest Urgent Care Center to treat a broken leg will be much more motivated to make a purchase than someone who is talking to a door-to-door magazine salesperson. Before you can convince potential customers that *your* widget is the best one out there, you may first need to convince them that buying a widget is a better decision than not buying anything at all.

Tip #31:
Think about How
Your Message is Framed

WHEN YOU LOOK AT a piece of art in a museum the underlying assumption is that the art must be "good" in some way, since, after all, it's in a museum. What if you saw the same piece of art being peddled on a street corner? How would this change of context change your perception of the artwork's value?

The Impact of the Frame

When implementing your marketing program, an important concept to keep in mind is the Frame. Why? Because an otherwise perfectly targeted and executed marketing message can be completely undermined by the wrong Frame.

What is a Frame? A Frame is the message that precedes your

message, or the context in which your message is viewed or received. The "set-up," if you will. The Frame shapes your prospect's assumptions and preconceived notions. A positive Frame increases the chances that your marketing efforts will succeed; a negative Frame can derail an otherwise great program.

Some Common Frames

Let's take a look at some of the Frames that may be impacting your marketing program:

- **Word of mouth** – Why is word-of-mouth advertising so successful? Because it's an incredibly powerful Frame. Your prospect is already "sold" before he picks up the phone.

- **Graphic design** – Your graphic design frames the context of your company's message. Does your design announce that you are you highly professional? Family-oriented? Hip and trendy? Guard against undermining your message with poor or inappropriate graphic design.

- **Print ads** – Print ads are framed by the editorial and advertising contexts of the advertising vehicle. Would you frame an ad for a steak dinner with an article about the benefits of vegetarianism – or in a publication targeting Hindus? Would you want that ad next to an ad for PETA (People for the Ethical Treatment of Animals)?

How is your message framed? To grow your business, pay close attention to this important element of your marketing program.

Tip #32:
Get Inside Your Prospects' Heads

WHEN SOMEONE IS LOOKING AT your marketing materials and deciding if they should call you, what might be running through their head?

Whether consciously or subconsciously, there are a few universal things that most of your prospects want to know. Here are two very important questions that your marketing materials must answer, and ways that you can make sure they do:

- **Can I Trust and Rely on You?** If you want people to fork over their hard-earned money to purchase your products or services, you must first build trust and establish credibility. People need to have confidence in you and your products. You can establish this by:

    o **Demonstrating your professionalism** – Including having well-written and professionally-designed materials. A website filled with errors, for example, does not build credibility.

    o **Providing testimonials** – Don't keep all that glowing praise from objective third parties to yourself.

    o **Making believable claims** – Hype and puffery does not build trust. Yours might not be the "most incredible offer in the history of the planet."

    o **Sharing your history** – If your company has been successfully serving your market for many years, you must be doing something right.

- **What's in It for Me?** How will your products or services simplify or improve my life, solve my problems or meet my needs? Speak to this unasked question by:

  o **Focusing on the benefits** of your product or service. As they say in sales, sell the sizzle, not the steak.

  o **Demonstrating the value** of what you have to offer.

  o **Offering to do the "hard work"** for your clients and let them take the credit (my ghost writing services are a great example of this).

  o **Making customers feel special** in some way.

Successful marketing materials answer these questions, appealing to the reader's needs and emotions to engage and sell.

Tip #33:
Market Results, Not Processes

WHAT KIND OF RESULTS do you think a pool cleaning service would get if they ran an ad with the following headline?

**Invite a Total Stranger into Your Backyard to
Brush, Vacuum and Dump Chemicals into Your Pool**

How about the following offer for a marriage therapist's services?

**Get 12 Weekly Sessions of
Emotionally Difficult Discussions for just $1,449!**

Or this attention-grabbing idea for a mortgage broker:

Let Us Bombard You with
Personal Questions and Never-Ending Paperwork

While these headlines are so surprising that they might get noticed, they probably would not result in a lot of sales. Why? Because they're focused on processes, not results. Although your potential customers might be interested in learning more about your processes at some point before they make their purchase decision, it's not likely to be the main thing that interests them. What they really want to know is this: What *results* can they expect to receive if they sign on the dotted line?

You've Got to Show the Value

By focusing on the *results* or *benefits*, you show people the *value* of what you're selling. Prospects need to see your offering as the answer to an essential need that they have. And they need you to spell this out for them clearly, as you can't count on them to figure it out themselves.

In the examples above, the pool cleaner's message should focus on how their service results in a sparkling clean pool. The marriage therapy will (hopefully!) result in a renewed connection with your spouse and a successful/happy marriage. And the mortgage broker can help you save money on your monthly mortgage, and/or give you the ability to purchase the home of your dreams.

A big mistake that I see in marketing materials written by people who are not professional marketing writers is a focus on features rather than benefits. Closely related to this is the problem of focusing on processes rather than results (i.e. benefits). By showcasing the results you show the value, which will help motivate prospective customers to make a purchase today.

Tip #34:
Sell to People, Not Businesses

IF YOU'RE SELLING PRODUCTS or services to businesses, there's a very important fact that you need to keep in mind: Businesses do not make purchase decisions – people do. You might think you're a "business-to-business" marketer, but what you actually should be is a "people-to-people" marketer. To sell to people rather than businesses, here are some important things you need to keep in mind:

- **Who are the people that you're selling to?** While your target market might be composed of "mid-sized manufacturing firms in Orange County," you need to know who the people are at these firms that will be making or influencing the purchase decision. Are you selling to the Purchasing Director, General Manager, Controller, CEO or Administrative Assistant? Will it be a group or solo decision?

- **What do you know about these people?** Can you make any generalizations about the demographics of the people you're marketing to, such as age, gender or educational level? What does their typical work day look like? What pressures do they face? What are their hot buttons?

- **What problems can you solve for them?** People buy solutions to problems. How is your solution better than your competitors'? When it comes to considering a product or service like yours, what issues are important to these people?

- **What are their hidden agendas?** The people who buy from you probably won't base their decisions solely on factors such as price, quality and service. They also have emotions, fears and hopes that drive their decisions. They're dealing with internal politics. They're worrying about how this purchase decision will affect their career.

They're wondering if buying from you will make their own job any easier. Sure they want to do what's best for the company – but they're also likely to do what's best for themselves as well. You need to keep all of this in mind, providing solutions that work on both the personal *and* business levels.

Tip #35:
Keep Your Message Focused

IT SLICES! IT DICES! It provides insurance for your business, clean carpets for your home and treats for your dog!

What's wrong with this message? It's trying to sell too many things at once. In fact, its message is so broad that it's confusing. What in the world is being sold here?

One of the keys to successful marketing is to focus your message. Don't try to promote too many things at once or combine too many ideas into one advertisement. Even if you have multiple product lines, it's not necessary to mention all of them in every communication.

To take a targeted approach and zoom in on what's important to your potential customers, before you start writing a marketing piece you should begin by answering the following three questions:

1. **What are you selling?** As I keep mentioning, always focus on the *benefits* of what you're offering. People want to know how your product or service will solve their problems, meet their needs or improve their life.

2. **Who are you selling it to?** Most products or services have more than one target audience. For example, my food allergy books are targeted at parents of children who have life-threatening food

allergies – but I also sell to people who buy the books as gifts, librarians, book stores and more. Who are you targeting in this particular marketing piece?

3. **What will appeal to these people?** Which of your products or services will be of the most interest to this target audience? What benefits should you emphasize? A caterer might highlight their "healthy food at reasonable prices" when marketing business lunches to corporations, but focus on "elaborately displayed gourmet food" when talking to brides-to-be.

Trying to be "all things to all people" can lead to confusion and/or an overly generic marketing piece. For greater success, keep your message appropriately focused.

Tip #36:
Develop Your Company's "Voice"

YOUR COMPANY HAS A "VOICE," and this voice is reflected in the writing style, tone and words used in your marketing materials. You're company's voice might be "corporate" or "professional." It might be "folksy," "warm and fuzzy," "high tech," "fun," or anything else. Whatever voice you use, it's important to ensure that (a) it will resonate with your prospective customers and (b) it is used consistently throughout your marketing materials.

To give you a feel for the difference that voice can make, I have taken a message that I wrote for a major player in the cut flower industry about product grading standards, and written it three different ways:

- **"Folksy" Voice (the actual text used in their brochure)** – No doubt you've heard the saying, "If it ain't broke, don't fix it." Here on the farm we have another saying: "If it ain't gorgeous, don't keep it."

We're so passionate about our quality standards that we'd rather send a marginal stem to the compost pile than ship it out to our customers.

- **"Corporate" Voice** – Quality control. It's at the heart of everything we do. And although creating high-quality flowers and greens starts out in the field, it's our very exacting grading standards that ensure consistent product for you. Any stem that doesn't meet the grade simply isn't shipped. We guarantee it.

- **"Obnoxious Teenspeak" Voice** – Hey Dude! How do we make sure you get flowers and greens that are totally sweet every time? We check them out. I mean, like, we check out every single stem to see if it totally rocks or if it sucks. And if it sucks, we chuck it onto a big compost pile instead of shooting it out to you. Cuz that would be bad. And we'd never do that.

As these examples demonstrate, voice really can make a significant difference!

Tip #37:
Create Irresistible Offers

IF YOU WERE SELLING $20 BILLS for $5 each, customers would be lining up to take advantage of your offer. Of course, you'd also quickly run out of money!

Offers (such as "money at a discount") are a time-tested way to turn your prospects into customers. Naturally, they work best when structured and presented in as enticing a manner as possible. Your "offer," however, is not just your "discount of the month" – it includes all of the elements that make up the deal you are presenting, such as the product or service itself, price, guarantee, terms, special promotions and so forth.

What Makes an Offer Successful?

The most successful offers are:

- **Unique** – Be fresh and different. Make your offer stand out from that of your competition.

- **Desirable** – Of course, a unique offer only works if it's something that members of your target audience actually want. If you're selling subscriptions to "Macho Man Magazine," "free lipstick" probably won't go over very well!

- **Easy** – If a person has to jump through hoops to take advantage of your offer, they're not likely to bother to do so.

- **Risk-Free** – Do whatever you can to minimize risk and sales pressure. For example, if the prospect can accept your offer without any obligation to make a purchase or commitment, say so.

- **Valuable** – Offer something with a high perceived value, especially in relation to your actual cost of goods and the potential lifetime value of the customer.

10 Offers that Don't Involve Discounts

Of course, there are a lot of options beyond "buy one get one free" and "order now to get 40% off." Plenty of proven offers leave your product's price intact, including:

1. **Money-Back Guarantee** – To remove all purchase risk.

2. **Extended Warranty** – To show that you'll stand behind your product for the long term.

3. **Payment Terms** – From "no payments for 30 days" to "we accept credit cards, debit cards and PayPal."

4. **Response Options** – Such as call, email, text, fax, fill in a form or request more information.

5. **Free Sample** – Try before you buy.

6. **Free Gift** – A promotional item, one of your other products, a product from a non-competitive business with whom you have created a cross-promotion, etc.

7. **Free Information** – Buy now and get a white paper, report or e-book.

8. **Free Consultation** – A "needs analysis" to determine if and how your product or service can meet their needs.

9. **Free Gift Wrap** – Can be much appreciated during the holiday season.

10. **Deadline** – Respond by a specified date to get a special incentive, such as a promotional item.

An offer says "when you pay us (or contact us, or give us your email address or whatever), here's what you'll get in exchange." A terrific offer – well-structured and well-presented – can be irresistible.

Chapter 5:
Develop Your
Writing Skills

"Writing – the art of communicating thoughts
to the mind, through the eye – is
the great invention of the world."
– Abraham Lincoln

HOW MUCH WRITING DO YOU do each day? Between emails, texts, letters, proposals and more, you probably do more writing than you realize. In business, the ability to clearly express yourself in writing can be a vital skill for marketing your business. Even if you plan to hire a professional marketing copywriter like me to write your formal marketing materials (something, of course, that I highly recommend), developing your own writing skills is still a good idea.

Tip #38:
Master these Easy Ways to Improve Your Writing

WORDS HAVE EXTRAORDINARY POWER. Good writing can help you communicate with both clients and prospects, expand your influence and increase your sales. Bad writing not only annoys and confuses, it also results in many missed opportunities.

Here are 10 easy ways to improve your writing:

1. **Identify your audience** – Knowing who you are writing for will help ensure that you use the proper tone and language.

2. **Stay on topic** – Identify the main points you want to convey, and then stick to them.

3. **Use an active voice** – This adds force and clarity to your writing, and makes it more interesting. For example, state that "Employees received bonus checks at the event" rather than "At the event, bonus checks were received by employees."

4. **Use strong verbs** – This is another way to make your writing more interesting. "Sales soared in June" is much more engaging than "Sales increased greatly in June."

5. **Avoid using jargon** – If it is necessary to use technical terms or acronyms, be sure to explain them. Don't assume that your readers know what you're talking about!

6. **Vary your sentence length** – Too many short sentences will make your writing seem choppy. Too many long sentences will make it hard to follow.

7. **Give examples** – Examples can make ideas easier to understand, personalize your writing and make it more accessible.

8. **Eliminate repeated words** – Vary your language. Avoid annoying your readers by using use the same words or phrases multiple times in one sentence or paragraph.

9. **Use transitions** – Transitional words and phrases, such as "therefore" or "in addition," help make one sentence or paragraph flow into the next.

10. **Trim it down** – Good writing is concise writing. Once your first draft is complete, take a hard look to see what needs to be either reworded or eliminated altogether.

Tip #39:
Avoid the Most Common Copywriting Errors

MARKETING WRITING – i.e. "writing to sell" – is very different than writing memos, essays and grocery lists. Once you succeed in getting a potential customer to open your brochure or visit your website, then what? Your website or brochure needs to be well-written! After all, it is the words that need to do the heavy lifting of *selling* your products and services, and *motivating* the reader to take action. If they don't, you're missing out on a lot of potential sales.

I'm frequently asked to review a company's "home grown" marketing materials and make suggestions for improvement. I often find the same errors. If you're taking the do-it-yourself approach to marketing writing (also known as "copywriting"), be sure to avoid these common blunders:

- **Hiding the Benefits** – Okay, I know I've mentioned this one before, but it always bears repeating. If you want to write to sell you *must* focus on the *benefits* that your product or service offers. Don't confuse features with benefits. All anyone cares about is "what's in it for me?"

- **Making Dubious Claims** – It only takes one unsubstantiated, hard-to-believe claim to wreck your credibility. No matter how tempted you are to claim that your new book is going to out-sell the Bible, don't do it!

- **Using Inaccurate Facts** – Check, check, and double-check all of the information you provide about your company and products. There's nothing more damaging than misrepresenting an important feature of your most popular product.

- **Sending Conflicting Messages** – If your first paragraph focuses on your "no payments for seven months" offer, your next paragraph shouldn't present your "30-day money-back guarantee." After all, anyone who takes you up on your offer will not be giving you any money for the first seven months – so at the 30-day point there will be no money to refund.

- **Focusing on Yourself** – One of the web developers I know likes to remind clients not to "we, we" all over their text. Take a look at how many of your sentences talk about "we" or "us" vs. "you" or "your." You should focus your text on the reader and his or her needs, not on company-indulgent posturing.

- **Keeping Your Product a Secret** – Many website home pages, for example, don't clearly announce what they're selling. If your company name is "ABC Marketing" and your headline is "Increase Your Sales!" it's hard to guess exactly what you do. Are you a marketing consultant, copywriter, SEO specialist, website developer, sales trainer or what?

- **Burying Key Information** – The key benefits and facts about your products and services should be front and center in your marketing materials. Don't expect potential customers to hunt for this information, because chances are they won't bother.

- **Using Inappropriate Vocabulary** – Your vocabulary needs to match the marketing piece's audience and purpose. Avoid using technical jargon for a non-technical audience, words like *existentialism* for a mass market audience and lots of contractions for a more formal piece.

- **Going On and On and On** – Your marketing materials should not look like short novels! Get to the point as quickly as possible. If you tend to be wordy, write the first draft and then edit out at least 25% of it to create draft two.

Tip #40:
Write Compelling Headlines

WHETHER YOU'RE PLANNING TO WRITE your own marketing materials or just want to understand how to properly evaluate what someone else has written for you, it's important to understand what makes a compelling headline.

Basic Functions of a Headline

A headline is essentially an advertisement for the rest of the piece. A headline's main function is to capture someone's attention and entice him or her to keep reading. It also needs to "select" the audience. For example, "Amazing Robotic Snow Blower Clears Driveways in Minutes" will attract a different set of readers than "Stay Cool During the December Heat Wave." Plus, if you're writing a print ad, the headline needs to deliver a message, as many people will read the headline and skip the rest.

Headlines that Make Me Cringe

One of my pet peeves is the use of "Welcome to ABC Corporation" or other non-benefit-oriented text as the headline on a website's home page.

Why does this drive me crazy? Because I hate to see such a complete waste of valuable online real estate. A website has about two or three seconds to grab someone's attention, convince her you're offering something that will solve her problems or improve her life, and persuade her to keep reading. The headline plays a huge role in this, and "Welcome to ABC Corporation" just doesn't cut it.

Questions to Ask Before You Start Writing

For marketing pieces, ask yourself: Who is your customer? What are the benefits of your product? Why will someone want to buy this product?

For articles, think about: Who is the reader? What information are you trying to convey in this article? What is the benefit of this information to the reader?

Common Headline Techniques

Here are some examples of different ways that you can approach the same subject matter:

- **Ask a question** – "What Makes Marketing Copy Effective?"

- **Make a statement** – "Effective Copywriting that Gets Results. Guaranteed"

- **Use a number** – "The 5 Keys to Effective Copywriting"

- **Tell "how to"** – "How to Write Marketing Copy that Gets Results"

- **Reveal "secret" information** – "Secrets of Effective Copywriting Revealed"

- **Use the word "free"** – "Free Report: The Secrets of Effective Copywriting"

- **Create urgency** – "Respond by March 31 to Learn the Secrets of Effective Copywriting"

- **Tell people what to do** – "Ensure Your Marketing Copy is Effective"

- **Present the "news" angle** – "New Technique for Effective Copywriting Increases Response by 200%"

- **Give the "best" or "worst"** – "Top Tricks for Effective Copywriting" OR "Avoid These Common Copywriting Blunders"

Tip #41:
Appeal to Readers' Emotions

IF YOU'RE WRITING A MARKETING PIECE, being truthful is a must. However, if all you do is present a list of straight-forward facts, you're not likely to make a lot of sales. Why? Because few people make purchase decisions based on facts alone. To actually sell your products or services you need to take those facts and communicate the impact – especially the emotional impact – that the purchase decision will have on the buyer's life.

Straight-Forward Facts vs. Emotional Appeal

So how do you transform dry facts into emotionally-appealing benefits? Take a look at these examples:

- **Charity**

  - **Fact:** We're asking for a $500 donation.

  - **Emotional Appeal:** Your $500 donation will ensure that 250 children in your area who would otherwise go hungry will enjoy a delicious and nutritious lunch every day next month.

- **Dog waste bags**

  - **Fact:** Each box contains 90 waste bags.

  - **Emotional Appeal:** Each box contains so many bags that you won't run out for months.

- **Medication warning**

  - **Fact:** Contraindicated for people who have diabetes.

  - **Emotional Appeal:** Can cause sudden heart failure in diabetics.

- **Dental office**

  - **Fact:** The office is open on Monday, Wednesday and Friday evenings as well as Saturday mornings.

  - **Emotional Appeal:** You won't have to miss work to see the dentist, thanks to our convenient evening and weekend hours!

- **Swimming pool cleaning service**

  - **Fact:** Incorrect pool chemistry can lead to the growth of micro-organisms and bacteria.

  - **Emotional Appeal:** Pool water can be very dangerous to your health. Our specialized training in pool chemistry means you can rest assured that your family and friends won't be hospitalized with water-borne illnesses after an afternoon in your pool.

For sales-oriented pieces, appealing to the reader's emotions communicates the "what's in it for me" factor in a way that will resonate.

Tip #42:
Avoid the Most Common Grammatical Errors

DO YOU HAVE A HARD TIME expressing yourself clearly in writing? If so, you're in good company. In addition to writing, I also do a lot of editing – and what I see is that many people do not know how to write grammatically correct sentences. To help make your writing flow more smoothly and correctly, here is a guide to some common grammatical mistakes. Keep in mind that, as these examples show, there is often more than one "right" way to write something.

- **Lack of subject/verb agreement –** When writing in the present tense, a singular subject requires a singular verb, and a plural subject requires a plural verb.

    o *Wrong:* Becky go to her dance class every Wednesday afternoon.

    o *Right:* Becky goes to her dance class every Wednesday afternoon.

    o *Wrong:* The neighborhood dogs barks all afternoon.

    o *Right:* The neighborhood dogs bark all afternoon.

- **Using run-on sentences** – Run-on sentences occur when what should or could be two separate sentences are put side-by-side without any punctuation or conjunction between them.

  o *Wrong:* Sam went to the store he bought some peas.

  o *Right:* Sam went to the store; he bought some peas.

  o *Right:* Same went to the store and he bought some peas.

  o *Right:* Sam went to the store. He bought some peas.

- **Using comma splices** – When two independent clauses (i.e. two sets of words that can each stand on their own as a separate sentence) are separated only by a comma, it's called a comma splice. Comma splices are always incorrect. Independent clauses should either be made into separate sentences, joined by a semicolon or joined by a comma plus an appropriate conjunction.

  o **Wrong:** It was a five-hour drive to Grandma's house, Jenna got very bored.

  o **Right:** It was a five-hour drive to Grandma's house. Jenna got very bored.

  o **Right:** It was a five-hour drive to Grandma's house; Jenna got very bored.

  o **Right:** It was a five-hour drive to Grandma's house, and Jenna got very bored.

- **Creating sentence fragments** – If your sentence is missing a subject, a verb or both, it is not a true and correct sentence – it is a fragment.

  o *Wrong:* The plumber that came to our house.

- o *Right:* The plumber that came to our house was punctual.

- o *Wrong:* Dancing in the streets.

- o *Right:* We were dancing in the streets.

- o *Wrong:* Because she was tired.

- o *Right:* Because she was tired, she went to bed.

- **Making vague pronoun references** – A pronoun (such as *he, she, it, this or which*) should clearly refer to the word or words it replaces.

  - o *Wrong:* When Bob and Pete went for a walk, he got thirsty.

  - o *Problem:* Who got thirsty – Bob or Pete?

  - o *Right:* When Bob and Pete went for a walk, Bob got thirsty.

  - o *Right:* Bob got thirsty when he went for a walk with Pete.

- **Misplacing modifiers** – Words that are meant to modify something else should be placed as close in the sentence as possible to the thing that they're modifying. Putting the modifier in the wrong place can change the meaning of your sentence.

  - o *Wrong:* Rebecca watched the sea lions out on the rocks wearing sun glasses.

  - o *Problem:* Who was wearing the sun glasses – Rebecca or the sea lions?

  - o *Right:* While wearing sun glasses, Rebecca watched the sea lions that were out on the rocks.

- **Using adjectives as adverbs** – An adjective is used to modify a noun; an adverb is used to modify a verb. It's important not to mix the two up!

  - *Wrong:* Herb did good on his math test.

  - *Problem:* "Good" is an adjective, but it is being used to modify a verb, "did."

  - *Right:* Herb did well on his math test.

  - *Wrong:* Leticia sings beautiful.

  - *Problem:* "Beautiful" is an adjective, but it is being used to modify a verb, "sings."

  - *Right:* Leticia sings beautifully.

  - *Another Possibility:* Perhaps you were actually trying to describe *what* Leticia sings, not *how* she sings. In this case, you can write: Leticia sings beautiful music.

Tip #43:
Learn the Proper Use of Punctuation Marks

ANOTHER THING I SEE A LOT OF in my editing work is incorrect use of punctuation marks. Here is a guide to some of the most common punctuation dilemmas, and some examples of correct punctuation mark usage for American English.

- **Semicolon vs. colon –** Semicolons are used either between two independent clauses (i.e. groups of words that can stand alone as a sentence) or to separate long or complicated items in a series that already uses commas. Colons are primarily used to introduce explanations, examples, series, lists or quotations. I like to think of semicolons as "separators" and colons as "announcers."

  o *Example:* Gerald arrived at the office just after dawn and stayed until well past the dinner hour; by the time he got home, he was exhausted.

  o *Example:* There are three things that Dawn loves to cook: Lasagna, pasta salad and chocolate chip cookies.

  o *Example:* There are three types of occasions for which Dawn loves to cook: For holidays, such as Valentine's Day and Christmas; during snow storms; and any time one of her four grown children, Derrick, Matilda, Mason or Daphne, come to visit.

- **Punctuation within quotation marks –** Commas and periods are always placed before the closing quotation mark. Question marks, exclamation points and dashes are put before the closing quotation mark when the punctuation applies to the quotation itself, and after when the punctuation applies to the whole sentence.

  o *Example:* "I wonder when the cherry blossoms will bloom," thought Leticia as she headed off to work.

  o *Example:* Martin screamed in exasperation, "I want to go home!"

  o *Example:* Do you agree with the saying, "A penny saved is a penny earned"?

- **Double vs. single quotation marks** – Double quotation marks are the standard form used for almost all occasions. Single quotations marks are generally only used to enclose a quotation within a quotation.

  - *Example:* "We had nearly reached the summit," Kevin explained, "when Christopher screamed, 'watch out for the tarantula!'"

- **Hyphenated adjectives** – Compound adjectives (i.e. adjectives that are composed of more than one word) are hyphenated. Single adjectives are not. When trying to decide whether or not to add a hyphen, make sure you're not including the noun in the hyphenated cluster of words.

  - *Example:* They met to discuss their five-week plan. ["Five-week" is a compound adjective that modifies the noun "plan."]

  - *Example:* The plan will take five weeks to implement. ["Five" is an adjective that modifies the noun "weeks."]

- **Using apostrophes to indicate possession** – Use an apostrophe when a word is possessive. When the word ends in an s (such as a plural), put the apostrophe after the s.

  - *Example:* This is the Scout's campsite. [This campsite belongs to just one Scout.]

  - *Example:* This is the Scouts' campsite. [This campsite is being shared by more than one Scout.]

  - *Example:* This is Russ' campsite. [This campsite belongs to Russ, and his name ends in the letter s.]

- **Using apostrophes to make contractions** – When making a contraction, use an apostrophe to replace the letters that are being removed.

  - ○ **Wrong:** Using *would'nt* for *would not*, as no letters were removed between the d and the n.

  - ○ **Right:** Using *wouldn't* for *would not*, as the letter removed was between the n and the t.

- **Using commas after introductions** – Introductory clauses, phrases and words provide background information or "set the stage" for the main part of the sentence. In most cases a comma should be placed after these types of introductions.

  - ○ **Example:** If she wants to get excellent grades, Becky must study every day.

  - ○ **Example:** A popular athlete, Tom was the top choice for Prom King.

  - ○ **Example:** Meanwhile, the basement filled with water.

Tip #44:
Proofread Everything

YOUR COMPANY'S WRITTEN WORDS "speak" for your business. Does your writing present a professional image, or are your materials filled with typos, misspellings, grammatical mistakes or other errors? No matter how good you are at what you do, documents containing obvious errors will erode your credibility…whether the errors are in your "formal" marketing materials or your "informal" emails and letters.

Here are some tips for effective proofreading:

- **Check your spelling** – At a minimum, be sure to use your word processor's spell check function! Although this won't catch all errors, it will catch many (for example, spell check won't notice the mistake if your typo is an actual word, such as "mop" instead of "map").

- **Read it out loud** – This is probably the most important step for successful proofreading. Hearing your document being read out loud makes it easier to notice awkward sentences, repetitive phrases, grammatical errors, typos that weren't caught by your word processing program and other mistakes.

- **Take a break** – If time permits, set your writing aside and revisit it later. You'll come back to the piece with fresh eyes and a new point of view.

- **Print it out** – Next, print out a hard copy of your writing and read it again. Sometimes you'll notice errors "in print" that you didn't see on screen.

- **Ask for help** – Once you are happy with your editing, ask someone who has a good understanding of spelling, grammar and punctuation to review the document for you. Even after checking and double checking, it's easy to miss an error in your own work that may be obvious to someone who is reading it for the first time.

Whenever you write something that's not just "for your eyes only," be sure that thorough proofreading and editing are integral parts of your writing process.

Chapter 6:
Improve Your
Marketing Materials

"When I write an ad, I don't want you to tell me that you find it 'creative.' I want you to find it so persuasive that you buy the product – or buy it more often."
– David Ogilvy

YOUR "MARKETING MATERIALS" INCLUDE everything from your website, brochure, social media pages, blog posts and promotional videos to your newsletter, print ads, sales letters, postcards, PowerPoint presentations and more. In fact, many if not most of the tactics you'll be using to implement your marketing strategies will require the use of some sort of marketing materials. To maximize the success of your marketing program, do everything you can to maximize the effectiveness of the marketing materials that support it.

Tip #45:
Start with an Evaluation

YOUR COMPANY'S MARKETING MATERIALS represent your firm. What message is presented? What image is projected? Can your marketing materials stand on their own? After all, when Joe Customer is surfing your website or reading your brochure, you're not there to augment your written words with a personalized sales pitch!

Take a Hard Look at Your Existing Materials

Pretend you're a potential customer and take a good look at all of your marketing materials. Ask yourself this important question: If your entire purchase decision was based on your website, brochure, ad or other marketing piece, would *you* do business with your company?

If your honest answer is "no," your first step should be to fix the basics. Make sure your marketing materials are:

- **Focused on the reader's needs** – Tell the reader how your product or service will solve their problems, meet their needs or improve their life.

- **Benefit-oriented** – Fill your marketing materials with benefit-oriented headlines, subheads and text.

- **Easy to scan** – If your materials look daunting to read, chances are no one will bother to read them. Break things up into short paragraphs, use subheads and bullet points, and put important points in bold type.

- **Well-designed** – Be sure that the colors, fonts, images and layout of your piece enhance the readability of your message, are pleasing to the eye and appropriate for the image you want to portray.

- **Error-free** – Errors reflect very poorly on your company and cast doubt upon the quality of your products or services. Your materials should be well-written and free of typos, grammatical mistakes and punctuation errors.

Remember, if your marketing materials are not effectively selling the reader on the benefits of your products or services – and if they're not motivating the reader to take action – you're missing out on a lot of potential sales.

Tip #46:
Develop Your Brand's Visual Image

WHEN YOU SEE MCDONALD'S golden arches, Nike's swoosh or Tiffany's distinctive blue packaging, you immediately know what company you are dealing with. These brands all have very strong and well-known images. However, even small companies should make the effort to create a brand image for their organizations. Luckily, it doesn't take a big budget to create a recognizable "look and feel" for your company – just some foresight and planning!

Evaluate Your Current Situation

Get out all of your company's printed materials – your business cards, letterhead, brochures, fliers, ads, newsletters, etc., as well as a printout of your website's home page – and spread them out on your desk. Take a good look at what you see. Is it visually obvious that all of these items are from the same company?

If not, you've got a problem that needs to be addressed.

Make Sure Your Customers Can Recognize You

A big part of branding is recognition. Having a "look" that you use across all of your marketing materials makes it easy for your customers and potential customers to recognize that a message is from your company.

Your brand's visual image is composed of three main elements:

1. **Your logo** symbolizes your company. Make sure it is easily recognizable and works well in a wide range of sizes and advertising media.

2. **Your color scheme** should be uniform throughout all of your materials, and appropriate for your goals. Some color combinations are relaxing and soothing, others suggest excitement and enthusiasm, while others project a very "corporate" image.

3. **Your overall "look"** (including colors, fonts, pictures, layout, etc.) needs to visually reinforce the feeling that you want your product or service to convey. A company marketing "mom's apple pie" to senior citizens will have a much different look than one selling the latest electronic gadgets to teenage boys.

It often takes multiple exposures to an advertising or marketing message before a consumer will decide to make a purchase or inquiry. If your materials are a mismatched hodge-podge of colors, designs and messages, it will be very difficult for you to build a recognizable presence in the marketplace.

Tip #47:
Format for Maximum Readability

YOU'VE TAKEN THE TIME TO CRAFT a beautifully-written letter or paid to have a professional copywriter write the words for your brochure or website. You're all set, right? Wrong! Having the perfect words isn't enough. Your finished piece needs to be formatted to be easy to read.

Sometimes people get so caught up in creating a certain image – or squeezing a lot of words into a limited space – that they completely lose sight of readability. However, unless yours is a completely visual message, it's important that people be able to read your words. Here's what you need to keep in mind:

- **Make it easy to scan** – People don't want to wade through what appears to be a short novel. If the mere sight of your written piece overwhelms the reader, you can bet he or she will quickly move on to something else.

  Recommendation: Put your headings and subheads in bold type, use bullet points, left justify your text (don't center everything) and break things down into short, easy-to-manage paragraphs.

- **Avoid giving readers a headache** – Have you noticed that an increasing number of websites are composed of tiny little white letters set against a black background? Ugh! Instant eyestrain.

  Recommendation: For maximum readability of any written piece (not just websites), stick with dark type on a light background, and don't use anything smaller than a 10-point font. This is especially important if you're targeting people who are over the age of 45.

- **Think about your font formats** – Sometimes it works to use special formatting to call attention to particular words, but if you're not careful you'll end up making those important words difficult to read.

  Recommendation: Go easy on your use of ALL CAPS, *italics*, <u>underlines</u>, Initial Caps and other special formats. These all work well on headlines and brief items, but should generally be avoided on longer passages.

If your written piece isn't formatted for maximum readability, there's a good chance it won't get read at all.

Tip #48:
Overcome the Difficulties of Marketing Intangibles

IF YOU'RE SELLING NECKLACES you can show a picture of the product and everyone will instantly know that you're selling necklaces. But if you're selling business services or life insurance or some other intangible product or service, explaining what you're offering and the benefits it brings isn't always easy.

How do you sell an intangible product or service, something that can't be seen or demonstrated? Here are five things you can do in your marketing materials that will help overcome the difficulties of marketing intangibles:

1. **Create trust** – Because your prospective customers can't take your product for a "test drive," finding ways to create trust is especially important. An accountant, for example, can use her marketing materials to create trust by listing her credentials, sharing testimonials, explaining her methodology and demonstrating her expertise.

2. **Humanize the benefits** – Make an emotional connection by demonstrating the benefits of what you sell. A wellness coach can show how good you'll feel after completing the program. A house cleaner can show how happy a working couple feels when they come home to a clean house. And so forth.

3. **Provide useful tools** – Help prospective customers see the value in what you offer by providing useful tools, such as an online calculator that shows people how much they need to save for

retirement or a checklist that helps them compare your service to your competitors'.

4. **Keep it simple** – Intangible products and services can be perceived as being difficult to understand. Unfortunately, a person who is confused will avoid making a purchase decision altogether. Do everything you can to make your product or service appear simple and understandable.

5. **Use metaphors** – If people do have a hard time understanding what it is that you're selling, try using a metaphor to describe your service or the problems it solves. For example, a mortgage broker can say that "refinancing your mortgage is like giving yourself a raise."

Tip #49:
Keep Your Text Reader-Focused

MANY COMPANIES MAKE THE common mistake of focusing their marketing materials exclusively on themselves. "We this," "our that," "we're proud of this," etc. While a certain amount of self-centeredness is appropriate, you've got to keep in mind that prospective customers don't really care about you. They care about themselves. And they want to know exactly what your company is going to do for them.

Same Information, Different Focus

Every page of your website or brochure (even the "About Us" page!) is another opportunity to show the reader how you are going to meet their needs. Yes, your marketing materials will be presenting a lot of information about you. The trick is to try to present this information so that it comes across as significant benefits for the reader.

Here are some "before and after" examples that demonstrate how messages can be reworded to make this happen:

- **Company-Focused:** We carry the largest selection of annuals, perennials and herbs in the state.

- **Reader-Focused:** To help you transform your yard into a garden paradise, Midtown Garden Center carries the largest selection of annuals, perennials and herbs in the state.

- **Company-Focused:** We are committed to simplifying our members' lives by providing personal assistance via the Internet and telephone.

- **Reader-Focused:** Work with a company that respects the value of your time! With XYZ Company the personal assistance you expect is always just a phone call or email away.

- **Company-Focused:** We are also a valuable resource for costume news and information through informative blog posts and social network discussions.

- **Reader-Focused:** Stay on top of current costume industry news and information with our informative blog posts and social network discussions.

- **Company-Focused:** We sell stylish, advertisement-free reusable grocery and tote bags.

- **Reader-Focused:** Why pay for the privilege of being a walking billboard for your local store? Now you can get great-looking, long-lasting reusable grocery bags without any advertisements at all!

Tip #50:
Build Credibility and Trust

WHICH COMPANY WOULD YOU rather do business with: An organization that has a positive reputation in the field and clearly stands behind its products, or a firm you've never heard of that doesn't even have contact information listed on its website?

No matter what's going on in the economy, your prospective customers are always going to want reassurance that you're reliable, stable, committed to quality and not going out of business tomorrow. Your marketing materials can play a big part in communicating this message.

Smart businesses start building credibility and trust from their very first contact with a prospective client. Their marketing materials include as much as possible of the following:

- **Contact information** – I, for one, will not do business with a company that won't even provide a telephone number. A mailing address is also reassuring.

- **Guarantee** – Your money-back guarantee should be prominently displayed. Keep it simple, and avoid watering it down with legal fine print. People want to know: Do you stand behind your products or not?

- **Testimonials** – What do others have to say about your products and services? When customers give you positive feedback, ask for their permission to include their remarks in your marketing materials (and get this permission in writing, such as via email).

- **Privacy policy –** If you're collecting any type of information online, a privacy policy is mandatory. Your offline customers might also want to know what you do and don't do with their data.

- **Ratings and awards –** Has your company won an award or received a favorable rating from an unbiased and recognizable source? Don't keep this information to yourself!

Of course, there's a lot more to building credibility and trust than simply providing information in your marketing materials. You also need to be honest in your business dealings, provide quality products or services and give top-notch customer service!

Tip #51:
Increase Sales by
Creating Anticipation

GOT SOMETHING EXCITING PLANNED for this weekend? Looking forward to the holidays? Anticipation can be a wonderful emotion, as it gets us focused on thoughts of the good things that are about to happen.

Of course, anticipation is not just for social events! It can also be used to increase your sales and improve your business' bottom line.

Maximize the Impact of Your Subject Line

When you use direct response mail or email as part of your lead generation program, one way to boost response is to use your subject line or outer envelope teaser line to create a sense of positive anticipation. Why? Because anticipation leads to engagement, and engagement leads to sales.

Here are four things you can do to build customer anticipation in your marketing messages:

- **Be intriguing** – Use an email subject line or outer envelope teaser line that makes the reader curious about the rest of the message. Some examples from work I've done include:

  - *Partition your servers while you're out at lunch*

  - *Think your portfolio is diversified? Think again.*

  - *The paradigm shift that will ignite your recruiting*

  - *Give your customers a 30% discount...courtesy of Uncle Sam*

- **Be recognizable** – For on-going campaigns, familiarity often creates anticipation. For example, many people tell me that they look forward to receiving my newsletter, *The Plumtree Marketing Minute*. When they see an email from Linda Coss with the familiar subject line, which always begins with "Newsletter," they look forward to opening the email and reading the latest issue.

- **Be generous** – Everyone loves freebies. If you're offering something for free – such as a free sample, trial, demo or gift – let the reader know right away! Just avoid using the word "free" in your email subject lines, because doing so can trigger spam filters.

- **Be exciting** – Sometimes creating anticipation can be as simple as changing the name of what you're offering. Which would you rather receive: A fundraising letter or a donor appreciation package? A paint store sales letter or a free guide to redecorating and upgrading your home without busting the budget? As you can see, what you call things can have a significant impact on the recipient's expectations and interest level.

Tip #52:
Motivate Prospects to
Take Action Now

TO INCREASE YOUR SALES you need to motivate your prospects to take the next step *now*, when they are most interested. After all, if they decide to wait until "later," later may never come. That's why creating a real sense of urgency in your marketing materials is so important. Fortunately, there are many ways to do this. For example, you can:

- **Make them really want it** – Show your prospects how your products or services will measurably improve their lives, either by giving them something wonderful that they truly want or by helping them avoiding something terrible that they don't.

- **State a specific deadline** – *Respond by 6:00 pm October 14th.* Mention that deadline in your email subject line or on your direct mail package's outer envelope. *The clock's ticking! Order before 6:00 Oct 14th and save!*

- **Imply time sensitivity in the offer name** – Advertise your *Early Bird Special*, *Memorial Day Sale*, etc.

- **Give an incentive** – Offer a free bonus that's tied to your deadline: *FREE SHIPPING if you order by 6:00 pm Oct 14th.*

- **Make it a limited offer** – Create urgency through scarcity. *Limited Time, Limited Quantities, Limited Edition, Only 3 Left in Stock.*

- **Use urgent wording** – Use your call to action to urge action: *Act Now, Don't Miss Out, Immediate Reply Requested, Call Today, Don't Delay.*

Of course, it's not enough to simply create a sense of urgency. You also need to ensure that potential customers have the information they need to make a buying decision, and that it's easy for them to act. Tell them exactly what they need to do next, and make doing this easy. For example, send them to a webpage where they can respond to your offer, put your phone number in big print, or include a map to your location.

Tip #53:
Prove Your Claims

WHAT DO THE FOLLOWING HEADLINES have in common?

Slash Your Energy Bill by $1000s

Look Visibly Younger in Just 10 Days

Accomplish Twice as Much in Half the Time

If you answered "they all make very strong claims," you're right! Whether they're in the headlines, subheads or text, most marketing materials contain claims. After all, you need to announce what it is about your product that makes it so desirable.

Keep it Believable

I've seen a lot of websites that are all breathless hype and puffery, with little to no proof that any of the wild claims are true. Am I *really* going to slash my energy bill by thousands of dollars? Have millions of people *really* watched their wrinkles magically disappear after using this product for just 10 days? I doubt it.

To be effective, your marketing materials must be believable. Otherwise instead of clicking the "Buy Now" button, your prospects will be clicking away to another site.

Provide Proof that Your Claims are True

Even if your claims pass the "believability test," you'll still want to back them up with some type of proof. Here are some ways to do that:

- **Free samples** – Let prospects try your product for free, so they can see for themselves that your claims are all true.

- **Testimonials** – It's not just you that's making these claims; others agree with them, too. Consider showing groups of testimonials in a list, sprinkling testimonials throughout your materials, using them as headlines or creating entire ads centered around these positive customer stories.

- **Third party ratings and awards** – If your product has won awards or received favorable ratings from reputable third party organizations, don't keep this information to yourself! After all, which sounds more credible – to say that "moms love it" or to say that your product "won the prestigious Mother's Choice award three years in a row"?

- **Comparisons** – Consider using a features comparison chart to compare your product to your competitors'. Or compare the results of using your product to the results of using the competitors' or to doing nothing at all.

- **Explanations** – Sometimes all it takes to prove a claim is to provide an explanation of the processes you follow or steps you take. For example, Enjoy Life claims their foods are "allergy friendly," and their website provides detailed information about the steps they take to ensure their foods are indeed allergen-free.

Tip #54:
Tout Your Value-Added Benefits

A WHILE BACK I SWITCHED telephone companies and signed up for a landline with what the customer service rep called "unlimited nationwide long distance calling." I frequently have lengthy calls with clients located in other states, and I've been very happy with the value that this calling plan provides.

Two years after I made the switch I was rather surprised to learn that my "unlimited nationwide long distance calling plan" also includes all calls to Canada. Evidently as a value-added benefit, my phone company throws this second nation in for free. Who would have guessed?

If a Tree Falls in the Forest...

This situation reminded me of the old philosophical question, "If a tree falls in a forest and no one is around to hear it, does it make a sound?" Only in this case I would ask, "If a company provides a potentially wonderful value-added benefit, but no one knows about it, does it actually do the company any good?" My answer is "No!"

What are Value-Added Benefits?

Many businesses – especially those in very competitive or commodity-like fields – attempt to differentiate themselves through the value-added benefits that they provide. These benefits can take many different forms, such as offering free gifts with purchase, enhancing product quality, adding features to the product or service, providing fast delivery and much more.

What Makes a Value-Added Benefit Strategy Effective?

From the marketing standpoint, the effectiveness of this approach is based on the prospect's or customer's perception of the value being received. If no one knows that the "valuable benefit" is being provided then the perceived value is zero, and the strategy is a failure.

Do your customers know about the value-added benefits that you provide? You should be touting the wonderful things that you do for your customers, not leaving them as a well-kept secret!

Tip #55:
Harness the Power of Testimonials

TESTIMONIALS ARE ONE OF the most effective ways to eliminate the fear or objections that people might have about doing business with you. If *you* say you are good, potential customers may not believe you. But when *others* say you are good, your credibility skyrockets.

What Makes a Good Testimonial?

The most effective testimonials are those that are:

- **Specific** – "Linda helped us to increase sales by over 50% in just 6 months" vs. "We like Linda's work"
- **Cite complete attributions** – "Jeffrey Nguyen, CEO, ABC Manufacturing Company, Los Angeles" vs. "Jeffrey, Los Angeles"
- **Use the customer's own words** – "I can't believe how well Linda took everything I gave her and turned it into gold!"

Where Can You Use Testimonials?

Once you collect testimonials (and obtain written permission to use them!) you can use them in all of your marketing materials.

For example:

- **Websites and brochures** – Use testimonials throughout your website and brochures to eliminate common sources of customer anxiety, such as price, quality and reliability. Place them in a side column, use them in your sales text, create separate "testimonials" pages, etc.

- **Emails** – Use relevant testimonials in the introductory letters that you email to prospective clients. Place testimonials in the first two inches (i.e. the part that displays in the preview panel) of sales-oriented pieces.

- **Direct mail** – Choose a testimonial that addresses a common buyer objection head-on and use it on the outside envelope, to help convince recipients to open the mailer. Or try using a powerful testimonial as the opening or P.S. of a direct mail letter.

- **Print ads** – You can create an entire marketing campaign built around "case study"-style customer testimonials. Include eye-catching photos of the customers using your products.

Testimonials let you stop bragging about yourself, and start letting others do the bragging for you!

Tip #56:
Showcase Your Successes with Case Studies

IN MARKETING, BELIEVABILITY IS always important. Prospective customers want reassurance that whatever you're selling really does work as well as you claim it does. That's why case studies – actual success stories about your products or services – can work so well.

Gain Instant Credibility

People like to identify with their peers. Case studies let your successes speak for themselves, and give your prospective clients a feel for how your products or services have benefited others like them. Plus, case studies give believable examples that bring your concepts to life.

Choose from Two Popular Formats

There are two popular formats for case studies:

- **"Factual" format** – The "factual" format is usually presented under subheads such as "Background," "Problem," "Solution" and "Result." These case studies are generally relatively brief and unemotional pieces that are especially appropriate for business-to-business marketing. They work because they explain, in purely factual terms, exactly how your company's products or services actually helped a particular customer.

- **"Story" format** – Case studies written in a "story" format read like magazine feature stories, and can be anywhere from a few paragraphs to a few pages in length. "Story" case studies are effective in both business-to-business and business-to-consumer marketing. They work because they're interesting and emotionally engaging.

Regardless of what format you use, the idea is not necessarily to present every little detail. Your goal is usually to tell enough of the story to get your point across, but not so much as to make the case study seem overly narrow.

Put Your Case Studies to Work

Where can you use case studies? In all of your marketing literature! Case studies can be effective in websites, brochures, press releases, articles, print ads, sales letters, social media, proposals and more.

Everyone loves success. Don't be shy about sharing yours.

Tip #57:
Improve Your E-Newsletter

WHAT'S THE DIFFERENCE BETWEEN an e-newsletter and a digital advertisement? Content. When properly written and executed, an email newsletter can help create customer loyalty, nurture sales leads and keep your business top-of-mind with customers and prospects alike. On the other hand, a poorly done e-newsletter can come across as spam – which can actually harm your business, creating ill will for your organization.

5 Key Things to Keep in Mind

So what are the keys to putting out a successful e-newsletter? You need to keep it:

1. **Short –** People are pressed for time. I keep the main articles in my newsletter to 300 words. If you want to write something longer – or if you want to include multiple articles – just put the first paragraph or so of each article in the email, and then let readers click through to a web page if they're interested in reading the rest.

2. **Relevant –** Before you begin to write, consider your audience. What interests them? What problems and challenges do they face? What can you write about that will truly speak to their needs?

3. **Informative –** A newsletter article is *not* the place to blatantly advertise your company's products or services (although you *can* do this in a side bar or other obvious ad). An article *is* the place in which to position yourself as an expert in your field by providing interesting and useful information. Articles about industry news and

trends, tips and tricks, case studies, helpful advice and so forth are all appropriate.

4. **Well written** – If writing is not your forte, hire a professional (such as me!) to do the writing for you. Double-check all facts and links, format it for readability and proofread it more than once.

5. **On schedule** – I recommend sending out newsletters every three to four weeks. But whatever schedule you choose, be sure you stick with it!

Tip #58:
Adjust Your Website's Focus

THERE ARE MANY FACTORS THAT differentiate a "good" website from a "bad" one, and many reasons why websites often fail to deliver the hoped-for results. When a website isn't working, the list of possible reasons include amateurish or inappropriate design, confusing navigation, lack of traffic, poorly targeted products, unappealing offers and inferior writing. Another possibility is that the website is focused on the wrong things.

Here are four subtle and not-so-subtle changes that can make a significant difference in your website's success:

1. **Focus on *visitors*, not *customers*** – Your customers are (hopefully) already sold on your company's products or services. Your visitors are not. Your home page or landing page should therefore focus on making an emotional connection with these people, showing them how you can meet their needs, and motivating them to become customers. Don't talk to your visitors as though they're already customers; they're not.

2. **Focus on *emotions*, not *logic*** – Even in the business-to-business world, most purchase decisions are not based entirely on logical, practical criteria. People buy things they want, that they believe will make them feel good (i.e. solve their problems or improve their lives), from companies or people that they trust. Be sure your website addresses the emotional, "feel-good" aspects of your offering.

3. **Focus on *marketing*, not *SEO*** – Now don't get me wrong – for most companies, Search Engine Optimization (SEO) is very important. But search engines don't buy your products; people do. So once you drive people to your website, make sure the words on your site are written for *them* and address *their* needs. Don't get so caught up with keywords that you forget to actually *sell* your products!

4. **Focus on *visit length*, not *number of visitors*** – If you drive 100,000 people to your website but they all leave within 2 seconds, what have you gained? Nothing. That's why you need to focus on enticing people to stay on your site long enough to digest your marketing message and then – hopefully – be motivated to take action.

Tip #59:
Learn to Create Successful PowerPoint Presentations

IF YOU OR YOUR TEAM MEMBERS are going to be giving face-to-face sales presentations, having a pre-set presentation can be extremely useful.

A great presentation is a masterful combination of three important elements: Content, design and delivery. For the design and delivery, Microsoft's PowerPoint can be a fabulous tool that helps you get your ideas across in an interesting and appealing manner. Unfortunately, the use of PowerPoint can also result in mind-numbingly boring presentations that are agonizing to sit through. Here are some proven tips for making your next PowerPoint presentation a success:

- **Take a minimalist approach to bullet points** – Try to keep it to just 3 or 4 bullets per slide, with a few words or a short sentence for each point. The goal is to just list key points – not to put your entire talk up on the screen.

- **Think about pacing and rhythm** – Vary the slide type and length. For example, don't show six bullet point slides or six bar graph slides in a row. Keep things interesting by mixing it up.

- **Give some thought to your graphics** – Choose one layout, color scheme and font to use throughout your presentation. Be consistent in your use of font sizes, too. Avoid switching between illustrations, color photos and black and white photos – the "mish mash" effect can be distracting.

- **Use informative headings** – Each slide's heading should instantly identify its main point, making it easier to follow along with your talk.

- **Proofread everything** – And then proofread it again!

- **Don't just read the slides** – Know your topic well enough to talk about it without reading. Your audience can read the slides themselves. They're looking to you to add something to the subject.

- **Show your passion** – Remember, a presentation is a marketing piece. This is true whether you're marketing information (such as a keynote speech) or trying to make a sale. Showing your enthusiasm for the subject will help keep your audience focused on what you have to say.

Tip #60:
Repurpose/Recycle/Reuse
Your Content

YOU MAY FIND YOURSELF PUTTING a great deal of time and money into creating original content. Whether you're creating written content such as articles and blogs, or multi-media content such as webinars and videos, finding ways to increase your return on investment for all of this content just makes good business sense.

Here are some ways that you can repurpose, recycle and/or reuse the content you create:

- **Repurpose your content for multiple mediums**

    o   Blog posts can be turned into podcasts and videos.

    o   Webinar content can be turned into white papers.

    o   FAQs can be the basis for "10 things you need to know"-type sales sheets.

    o   Articles can be posted to article distribution sites.

    o   Brochure pdf files can be posted on document sharing sites.

    o   Customer testimonials can be used in your website, brochures, sales letters and media releases.

- **Recycle your content with different "story angles"**

    o   Articles can be rewritten for different audiences. For example, "Optimizing Your Law Firm's Website" can be rewritten with pertinent examples for accountants, chiropractors or auto repair shops.

- o Case studies can be morphed into media releases based on the "news angle" of the story.

- **Reuse your content on multiple platforms**

  - o Webinar slide decks can be posted on slide sharing sites, so that today's presentation has visibility for years to come.

  - o Newsletter articles and media releases can be used as blog posts.

  - o Images of your product can be used to create engaging Pinterest pinboards.

- **Repackage a few existing items into one new item**

  - o A series of articles or blog posts can be aggregated and turned into an eBook, white paper or free report.

  - o A series of videos can become an online course.

Bottom line: Once you get into the mindset of repurposing, you'll find numerous ways to make the most of the content you create.

Tip #61:
Remember to Ask for the Sale

YOU'VE SEEN ADS LIKE IT BEFORE. There's an attention-grabbing headline, beautifully-designed graphics and well-written text that clearly communicates the benefits of the product or service offered. All that's missing is a suggestion as to what you should do next. They forgot to ask for the sale!

What is a "Call to Action"?

A call to action is a phrase or paragraph that asks for the sale or requests that the reader do something. It's the part of the marketing piece that tells the reader what to do next: call now to place an order, click here to get a free report, email for more information, enter a survey to win a prize, subscribe to an online newsletter, etc.

Never assume that your potential customers will know why they should act, what they should do or when they should do it!

Tell Them Exactly What to Do

Each of your marketing pieces should include a call to action (which may be mentioned multiple times, not just at the end) that ties in with the piece's overall goals. If your goal is to sell, don't ask readers to call for more information – ask them to purchase your product today. And always keep your instructions simple and clear to make it easy for the reader to respond. Should they call, fax or email? Do they need to click through to something, fill out a short form or take some other action? What exactly should the reader do?

Of course, it's not enough to tell the reader what they should do. You also need to tell them why they should do it and why they should do it now. But the bottom line is, if you're not asking for the sale, don't expect to get it!

Chapter 7:
Pay Attention
To the Details

*"People don't care how much you know
until they know how much you care."*
– John C. Maxwell

IN BUSINESS YOU NEED TO pay attention to the details, and these "details" include all aspects of the customer service you provide. Although you might not think of customer service as part of "marketing," as far as I'm concerned it is. Why? Because every interaction that a customer has with your organization is an opportunity for you to reinforce your brand message, make a positive impression and convince them that they should continue to do business with you in the future.

Tip #62:
Build Customer Loyalty

MOST BUSINESSES DEPEND ON repeat orders from existing clients to get and remain profitable. Why? Because the cost of acquiring new customers can be quite a bit higher than the cost of keeping the customers that you already have.

Even Happy Customers Aren't Necessarily Loyal Customers

Today it is easier than ever to "find a better deal" elsewhere. Loyal customers understand the intrinsic value of dealing with your company, and aren't tempted to jump ship the moment another offer comes along.

A typical business only hears from a tiny percentage of unhappy customers. The rest simply take their business elsewhere... or announce their dissatisfaction to the world through social media sites, and *then* take their business elsewhere.

Here are 25 things you can do to help ensure your clients are satisfied, feel appreciated and want to continue buying from you:

1. **Be enjoyable to work with**

2. **Understand – and meet – their needs**

3. **Solve their problems**

4. **Differentiate yourself from your competition**

5. **Convey your product or service's value**

6. **Deliver more than they expect**

7. **Simplify the buying process**

8. **Make realistic promises**

9. **Manage expectations**

10. **Be dependable and reliable**

11. **Be consistent**

12. **Be proactive**

13. **Keep in touch**

14. **Make it easy for customers to communicate with you**

15. **Be responsive on social media**

16. **Encourage feedback**

17. **Address complaints quickly – and turn them into opportunities**

18. **Be flexible when issues do come up**

19. **Express your gratitude**

20. **Show empathy**

21. **Provide valuable resources**

22. **Share your expertise**

23. **Make loyalty-building a team effort**

24. **Reward employees for providing excellent customer service**

25. **Measure everything and use the data for improvement**

Many companies have formal customer loyalty programs that reward customers for sticking around. These programs can be very successful, but they're not a substitute for creating a customer experience that makes people *want* to do business with you again.

Tip #63:
Create Positive Expectations

TWICE A WEEK I HEAD TO the gym for an early morning workout. On most days the guy behind the counter rarely manages to say "good morning" as he scans my membership card. Once, though, there was someone else handling check-in. This guy scanned my card, glanced at the computer to see my name, looked me in the eye and then offered a hearty *"Enjoy your workout, Linda!"*

And, I must say, after his greeting set such a strong positive expectation, I *did* enjoy my workout much more than usual.

Expectations Make a Difference

This got me thinking about the importance of creating positive expectations for our customers. A person who *expects* to have a positive experience will be looking for validation of this expectation. Unfortunately, the opposite is also true.

How can you create positive expectations for your clients? Here are a few ideas:

- **Website** – A well-designed, well-written website implies that yours is a professional, well-run company. Benefit-oriented text sets the expectation that your product is going to solve the readers' problems or improve their lives in some way.

- **Graphics** – The colors, fonts and pictures on everything from your marketing materials to your in-store signage create an impression as well. Think carefully about the mood/image that is created, and the expectations that your potential customers are likely to form based on this.

- **Staff** – As my gym example shows, even seemingly trivial customer interactions are important. Take a look at everything from how you answer the phone to your sales peoples' body language.

- **Product Names** – Product names can create expectations, too. For example, sitting in my pantry is the box of "Special K Chocolatey Delight" cereal that my son picked out. As a chocolate lover, the words "Chocolately Delight" definitely create a positive expectation for me!

Tip #64:
Put Out the Welcome Mat

IN THE BIG PICTURE, "MARKETING" encompasses all of the interactions that your customers and prospects have with your brand. Unfortunately, many businesses get so focused on the obvious "touch points" in the sales and marketing process (such as their website, marketing materials and sales meetings) that they lose sight of other important aspects of their potential customers' experience.

What does your company do to welcome people to your brand? Do you put out an inviting "welcome mat," or do you make prospects wonder why they bothered to call?

Help Customers Anticipate a Great Experience

Ideally your marketing materials will motivate prospective customers to take action. But once they take action, then what? I recommend you give some thought to creating a purposeful beginning to your customers' interaction with your brand, to help them anticipate the positive experience that your organization offers.

How Other Organizations Welcome their Customers

To help you start thinking about what you can do to "put out the welcome mat," here are some examples of what others are doing:

- **Fine dining** – Ambiance is often key at restaurants. White table clothes, fresh flowers, beautifully worded menus and other details all set the tone when customers first arrive.

- **Churches** – Why wait until people step in the door to give them a warm greeting? Many religious organizations now have greeters in the parking lot, to make people feel welcome from the moment they arrive.

- **Pet stores** – Some pet stores encourage customers to bring their furry companions shopping with them, welcoming these special guests with fresh water and treats.

- **Home builders** – The sales offices at model homes – with their maps, pictures and homey decor – help set the mood before your tour even begins.

When brainstorming things your company can do to make customers feel welcome, don't overlook the obvious. For example, make sure your telephone is answered by a human being, with a warm and welcoming voice, email inquiries are responded to promptly and customers are greeted with a smile and "hello" when they walk in your door.

Tip #65:
Help Your Clients Succeed

IF YOU'RE LIKE MOST BUSINESS PEOPLE, you spend a lot of time thinking about ways to reach your business' goals. The question is: What are you currently doing to help your clients reach *their* goals – besides selling them your cost-saving/performance-improving product or service?

If you're a business-to-business marketer, you should be doing all you can to help your clients succeed. After all, successful customers are the ones that pay their bills and come back to order more!

Here are some things you can do to promote your clients' businesses:

- **Referrals** – Keep your eyes and ears open for people and businesses that can benefit from your clients' products and services, make those introductions and then follow through to ensure the connection is made.

- **Website links** – Add a links page to your website, and list your clients here. Instead of talking about the work *you* do for these companies, use the links page to showcase *their* products and services.

- **Newsletter mentions** – If you put out a regular newsletter, include a "customer spotlight" section so you can easily advertise your clients' business to your entire distribution list.

- **Literature distribution** – If you have a retail store, buy a literature display rack and use it to display your clients' brochures.

- **LinkedIn recommendations** – Post positive reviews of your clients on LinkedIn and other business networking sites.

- **Blog topics** – Got a blog? Devote one post a week to highlighting your clients' products, specials, upcoming events, etc.

In many ways your business' financial success is dependent on your clients' financial success. Your efforts to help your clients success will help reinforce (i.e. "market") the value of doing business with you.

Tip #66:
Knock Their Socks Off

YOU'RE NOT IN BUSINESS TO sell products or services. You're in business to solve your customers' problems or improve their lives in some fashion. And if you can do this in such a way that it takes your customers' experience from "okay" to "wow," you'll end up with very loyal customers who will happily recommend your company to their friends and associates as well.

Much of Marketing is about Differentiation

You need to differentiate yourself from your competitors as well as from all of the other choices that your potential clients have, including the "do nothing" option. One way to do this is to expand your focus beyond your product or service, taking a close look at the entire *brand experience* that you present.

How can you take your brand experience from "okay" to "wow!"? Here are a few ideas:

- **Remember your customers' names** – This might seem basic, but it really makes a huge difference. And if your business is primarily conducted over the telephone, learn to recognize their voices (or use caller ID!) when they call.

- **Use the news** – Scan the news, watching for articles that would be of interest to your clients. Pop these in the mail with a handwritten note, possibly even highlighting the portion of the article to which you want to call attention.

- **Do the unexpected** – Bring in lunch for the whole staff at an important client's office. Talk an existing or potential client *out* of a purchase, if you feel the purchase wouldn't be in their best interest (I do this all the time). Add a "joke or inspirational message of the day" to your email signature block. Send postcards in honor of wacky holidays.

- **Be fun to deal with** – Smile. Joke around. Don't take yourself or your business too seriously. Be a dependable source of positive energy, a "ray of sunshine" that clients look forward to calling or visiting.

Disney's hotel housekeepers sometimes tuck guests' dolls and stuffed animals into bed, creating a "magical" moment when the families return. Some online shoe retailers eliminate buying risk by providing free shipping for both purchases *and* returns. What can you do to knock *your* customers' socks off?

Tip #67:
Master Email Etiquette

HOW MANY EMAILS DO YOU SEND and receive every day? For many of us, email is an indispensable part of doing business. Make the most of email's possibilities by ensuring that everyone in your organization is familiar with these basic "rules" of proper email etiquette:

- **Reply promptly** – Every in-bound message from a customer or prospect is a chance to demonstrate the high level of customer service that your organization provides. Always reply, and reply promptly.

- **Include a copy of previous emails** – When replying to emails, include the entire message stream. Not everyone can remember every communication that they have had, and this small courtesy makes it easy for the recipient to quickly refresh their memory.

- **Write meaningful subject lines** – A subject line that clearly announces what the email is about makes it easy for the recipient to distinguish important messages from spam, and also makes it simple to find the message in your history file if you need to refer to it at a later date.

- **Be polite** – Every message that you send is a reflection on you and your company. Use "please" and "thank you," avoid using all capital letters (the email equivalent of screaming), and don't write anything that you might later regret.

- **Pay attention to formatting** – The structure and layout of your emails will have a big impact on their readability. Use short paragraphs, and insert blank lines between paragraphs. Left justify your text (vs. centering, which is harder to read), use bullet points and so forth.

- **Use Standard English** – Improper spelling, grammar and punctuation not only give a bad impression of your company, but can also change the meaning of your message. Re-read your text before hitting the "send" button to be sure it is error-free.

Chapter 8: Focus on the Follow-Through

"If you are not taking care of your customer, your competitor will."
– Bob Hooey

IF YOUR MARKETING EFFORTS are successful, you will have a steady stream of leads and prospects. How you treat these leads and prospects will have a big impact on how many of them turn into customers. And how you treat your customers will have a big impact on how many of them choose to buy from you more than once. As part of your business growth efforts, make focusing on the follow-through part of your marketing plan.

Tip #68:
Sell the Buying Experience

NO MATTER WHAT KIND OF BUSINESS you are in, you're not only selling solutions – you're also selling an *experience*. I'm not just referring to the experience that your product or service itself will bring to the customer. You're also selling the experience of purchasing that product or service.

The question is: Are you selling a positive, enjoyable experience, or is dealing with your company a major turn-off?

"Marketing" Doesn't End When the Customer Contacts You

Although the goal of your marketing program may be to get people to pick up the phone, visit your website or stop by your store, what happens when they do so is a critical part of the sales and marketing process.

Many organizations seem to overlook the fact that customer service can be the point of differentiation between a successful company and one that doesn't last for long. After all, who would you rather buy from: A product or service provider that acts as though they're doing you a favor by selling you something, or one that bends over backwards to make the buying experience enjoyable for you?

Make it Easy to Buy from You

Do everything you can to make the experience of buying from you easy and painless. Answer your phones, return calls promptly, have a clear and easy-to-navigate website, simplify your ordering process, hire enough staff members to handle your customer volume, have a clean and attractive store.

Make it Fun to Buy from You

You're selling an experience. What can you do to make this experience fun for your customers? Some sporting goods stores add climbing walls, shopping centers host live musicians and pet stores hold regular "yappy hours." These things really up the "fun factor." But even service providers can make the buying experience more enjoyable, just by projecting a positive and fun attitude.

The bottom line is, if people don't enjoy doing business with you, they'll take their business elsewhere. So when evaluating your marketing efforts, don't forget to take a close look at the overall experience you provide for your clients.

Tip #69:
Find Excuses to Say "Thank You"

WHAT ARE TWO SIMPLE WORDS that you learned when you were young that are always well-received? "Thank you." Just like knowing when to say "I'm sorry," knowing when to say "thank you" can go a long ways towards creating positive and lasting relationships with your clients.

In fact, I'd like to suggest that you go so far as to look for "excuses" to express your thanks. Whether you simply say "thank you," or you send a thank you note, gift or e-card, the important thing is to be sincere and let people know how much you truly appreciate them.

- **Thank people for meeting with you** – Time is valuable. When people choose to spend their time meeting with you, be sure to drop them a thank you note after the meeting is through.

- **Thank people for doing business with you** – Each time someone does business with you, consider sending a short, personalized "thank you" via email or mail.

- **Thank people for providing feedback or suggestions** – Whether the feedback is positive or negative, express your gratitude for the input, and let the person know how their suggestion will be used.

- **Thank people for complimenting you** – It feels great when someone appreciates the good work that you have done. Share the good feelings with a note thanking the compliment-giver for taking the time to make your day.

- **Thank people for being extremely helpful** – When a client has gone out of their way to provide support for you on a project, let them know how much this meant to you.

- **Thank people for referrals** – Word-of-mouth advertising is the best form of advertising available. When someone sends new customers your way, be sure to express your appreciation.

- **Thank people for timely payments** – Accounts receivable issues can be a real problem for many businesses. When clients do pay in a timely fashion, send them a quick email to let them know their timeliness is appreciated.

Tip #70:
Learn How to "Market" Difficult News

IT'S A FACT: SOONER OR LATER you'll have to deliver difficult news to a client. Perhaps you made a mistake or missed a deadline. Maybe a delivery will be delayed, prices have gone up or credit has been denied.

Whatever it is, how you present the news (i.e. how you "market" it) can have as big an impact as the news itself.

Dealing with problems is never easy, but how you deliver difficult news – and of course follow up by delivering solutions – can make a big difference in your client relationships. Here's what you should do:

- **Assess the situation** – To whom should you be delivering the news? What impact will this news have on the customer and their business? If there is a problem, what will it likely take to convince the customer that the situation is contained or under control?

- **Tell the client as soon as possible** – Don't try to hide the situation. "I have something to tell you that is not what you're expecting to hear."

- **Accept the blame and apologize** – If you or your company has done something wrong, now's the time to admit it. Whether or not it was your fault, a heartfelt apology will demonstrate your sincerity and concern.

- **Empathize** – Let the client know that you understand what an inconvenience (or serious problem) this situation is for them.

- **Present solutions** – Focus on what you can do to alleviate the situation for your customer. Be prepared to offer what you see as the best possible solutions.

- **Follow up** – Stay in close contact with the customer until you know that the problem has been resolved to their satisfaction.

Finally, don't forget to ask for the client's continued support. "Mary, can I count on you to accept my apology and continue to work with me to keep things moving forward?" This often-neglected step can help save the relationship in spite of the current glitch.

Tip #71:
Avoid Sabotaging
Your Sales Efforts

DOES YOUR COMPANY HAVE A "Sales Prevention Department"? Even if you don't have a formal department with this name, if your organization's actions are preventing sales then the net effect is the same. Be sure to avoid these surprisingly common behaviors that can sabotage your sales efforts:

- **Acting rude and unprofessional** – This is probably the easiest, most sure-fire way to prevent sales. Have you ever walked out of a store (or hung up the phone) because the sales staff was obnoxious? I have. And so will your potential customers.

- **Avoiding marketing** – A successful marketing program will introduce potential customers to the benefits of doing business with you and produce a steady stream of qualified leads. If you're not marketing, your sales pipeline will dry up.

- **Wasting sales leads** – Once you get these precious leads, what do you do with them? I'm amazed that companies will go to trade shows, run ads, attend networking events, entice people to join their mailing lists, etc. – and then drop the ball once the leads come in. What a waste of time, money and effort! All leads should be followed up on as soon as possible, preferably within 24 hours.

- **Ignoring customers' needs** – What are your customers looking for? Better, cheaper, faster? A high-end luxury experience? Someone to hold their hand through a high-tech process? 24/7 access to your staff? Whatever it is, you've got to deliver. If you don't, your competition will.

Hopefully you don't recognize your company in this list. But if you do, now's a good time to make some changes!

Tip #72:
Make it Easy for Prospects
To Say "Yes"

MUCH OF YOUR MARKETING PROGRAM is probably geared towards attracting prospective clients to your business. Getting them in the door (or on the phone or at your website), however, is just the first step. After that you need to move your prospects along the sales process, making it as easy as possible for them to make the purchase decision.

Unfortunately, many companies lose out on a lot of business because they fail to recognize and remove sales obstacles. Don't let this happen to you. Here are some of the things that you can do to make it easy for prospects to say "yes":

- **Establish credibility** – Provide helpful information about your company, product or expertise. Avoid using "hype" in your marketing materials. Share testimonials from previous, happy customers.

- **Demonstrate value** – Make the benefits and value of your product or service clear. When possible, use specifics, such as "increase your profit by 25%," "save over $80 per day," "keep your network running 24/7," etc.

- **Offer a free taste** – Many cookbook websites offer free recipes. Why? Because nothing sells cookbooks like sample recipes. People cook up one or two, see that the recipes really are delicious and then purchase the book. What kind of a "free taste" can you offer?

- **Give a guarantee** – Your prospective customers want to know that you stand behind your product or service. A money-back guarantee can take the risk (or perceived risk) out of a purchase.

- **Make obtaining results look easy** – Getting the desired results with your product or service should appear as easy as possible. People are busy, and they demand simple solutions to their problems. If using your product or dealing with your company appears to be a hassle, you'll lose the sale.

- **Examine your website** – Is it easy to navigate? Is your contact information easy to find? Do you provide multiple ways for customers to contact you (phone, text, fax, email, snail mail, social media)? If you're selling something directly from your website, is your order information easy to find and your shopping cart simple to use?

Identify and eliminate every sales obstacle you can, and start making more sales!

Tip #73:
Avoid Following Bad Advice

BLOGS, ARTICLES AND WELL-MEANING business associates are often full of marketing advice. Unfortunately, some of it is not just bad advice, it's terrible, potentially damaging advice. Here's a round-up of some of the outrageously bad marketing advice that I've seen or heard:

- **You absolutely must be on [name of social network goes here]** – Maybe you should and maybe you shouldn't. There is no "one size fits all" social media marketing strategy that works for all businesses.

- **Pinterest only works for consumer brands that sell fashion or food** – Actually, a lot of companies in other categories are successfully using this very visual social media site. They're sharing infographics, company photos, tips and tricks, user-generated content and more.

- **If you start blogging, your audience will naturally find you** – Don't bet on it. To gain an audience you'll need to promote your blog.

- **Every legitimate business needs a printed brochure** – Printed brochures are great for trade shows and expos, business networking meetings, in-person sales calls, direct mail and more. But for many businesses they're completely unnecessary.

- **If you get to page one of Google you'll be successful** – Although page one listings are certainly helpful, once prospects click through you need to have a website that actually *sells* your products or services. And page one listings are useless if they bring in people who aren't looking for the things that you're selling (for example, if you're selling an egg-free cookbook and Google lists you as #1 for "egg recipes").

- **Business-to-business marketers don't need a mobile-ready site** – According to the Pew Research Center, back in 2013, 63% of adult cell owners used their phones to go online and 34% of cell internet users went online *mostly* using their phones. You can bet the numbers have gone up since then. No business can afford to ignore mobile.

Chapter 9: Conclusion

"We are what we repeatedly do.
Excellence, then, is not an act, but a habit."
– Aristotle

WHETHER YOUR BUSINESS IS large or small, marketing is an on-going process. If you're the owner of a small business you probably wear a lot of hats. Sometimes one of the hardest things to do is to carve out the time to deal with marketing – especially when things are going well and you're up to your eyeballs in work. Which is why I'll conclude this book with two final tips: Be consistent, and don't forget to show up!

Tip #74:
Be Consistent

WHEN IT COMES TO EXERCISE, everyone knows that consistency is key. While occasional exercise is better than none, it takes consistency to get and stay fit. Marketing is a lot like exercising. If you want to reach your goals, it's not enough to simply *plan*. You also need to consistently *do*. Consistency is key.

In fact, to get the best results, you need to be consistent and have:

- **Consistent branding** – To make sure that your customers can recognize you, all of your marketing materials need to have a unified look and feel.

- **Consistent messaging** – Once you have determined the main things that you want to communicate to your prospects, your written marketing materials *all* need to reflect this.

- **Consistent strategy** – In marketing, a prospect often needs to see or hear your message many times before he or she will take action. That's why if your strategy is to use a particular marketing vehicle, you need to stick with that vehicle long enough to give it a fair chance.

- **Consistent action** – Making things happen requires action. Once you have created a marketing plan, you need to schedule time to put your programs in place. Put it on the calendar. Literally. Pressed for time? Find ways to simplify your marketing efforts, such as writing four issues of your monthly newsletter at once and then putting the publication on auto-pilot for the quarter.

- **Consistent follow up** – They say that showing up (i.e. consistent action) is half the battle. If your marketing program is designed to bring in leads, then following up is the other half!

- **Consistent quality** – If the quality of your product or service itself isn't consistent, you can bet that your customers will be extremely consistent about quickly spreading the bad news.

Tip #75:
Don't Forget to Show Up

WOODY ALLEN ONCE SAID THAT "80% of success is showing up." Or, as my brother used to say, "you snooze, you lose." After all, it's hard to catch the opportunities if you're not there when they arise!

Where Should You Show Up?

Don't underestimate the importance of SEO (Search Engine Optimization) in the virtual world, or the importance of talking to people in the physical world. You should show up wherever your clients are, such as:

- In online search results

- At business networking events

- In social media

- At trade shows

- When people reach out to you

How Should You Show Up?

There's more to "showing up" than just going through the motions or walking in the door. You need to:

- **Show up fully –** Be fully present physically, mentally and emotionally. And when your business "shows up," be sure that its presence is a positive reflection on your brand as well.

- **Show up consistently –** The old saying, "out of sight, out of mind" is very true. If you join a business networking group, plan to attend every meeting. If you put out a monthly newsletter, make sure it goes out once a month. And if you decide to participate in social media, remember that this takes more of a commitment than just logging in once a week.

- **Show up positively –** People do business with people and businesses that they like and trust. Be the type of positive person and business that others want to associate with.

The truth is, I often get business simply because I answer my phone and return emails promptly. Customers tell me, "I reached out to several copywriters, but you got the job because you're the only one who immediately replied." If you don't show up, somebody else will.

About the Author

LINDA COSS IS A FREELANCE MARKETING WRITER (also known as a marketing copywriter) who helps organizations in a broad array of industries reach their goals. Clients across the country appreciate her ability to write targeted and effective marketing materials that don't merely inform – they appeal to the reader's needs and emotions to engage and sell.

Known for writing high quality materials that are done right the first time, Linda brings two decades of marketing experience to every assignment. Her areas of expertise include writing the text for websites, brochures, newsletters, articles, blogs, sales letters, postcards, print ads, press releases and more.

To learn more about how Linda can help your business, visit her website at www.PlumtreeMarketingInc.com.

Of course, Linda also welcomes your feedback and dialogue about this book. You can reach her at Linda@PlumtreeMarketingInc.com.